Edition

WRITING WORKSHOP

EXAMINATION LEVEL CSEC ENGLISH

TERRY NISBETT

EXAMINATION LEVEL CSEC ENGLISH

Writing Workshop

Copyright © Theresa Nisbett 2009

Published by
Theresa Nisbett
Nisbett Communications
P.O. Box 890
Basseterre
St. Kitts

All Rights Reserved. No part of this work may be reproduced, transmitted, stored or used in any form or by any means graphic, electronic, mechanical, photocopying, recording, scanning or otherwise without the written permission of the publisher.

First printed 2013

ISBN: 978-976-95542-0-7

© Theresa Nisbett, 2009
Suncrest
Basseterre, St. Kitts
Phone 869.465.1668 • Mobile 869.664.2728

For my children

Tamu Petra Browne and Brett Nisbett

whose enthusiasm and fearlessness I try to emulate.

CONTENTS

Preface	vii
1. Persuasive Writing	**1**
Getting Started	1
Logic and reason	5
Prioritise	5
Developing a paragraph	7
Getting the flow	10
Suggestions for openings	11
Sample persuasive writing	15
Letters to the Editor	16
Sample letter to the Editor 1	17
Sample Letter to the Editor 2	19
Speech	21
2. Short Story	**31**
Elements	31
Plot	31
Setting	32
Characters	33
Dialogue	33
Conflict	34
Storyline	34
Working With The Elements	37
Creating a character	37
Dialogue	38
Setting	40
Plot	41
Responding to stimulus material	47
Openings and closings	52
Closing with a twist or surprise ending	53
Sample Short Story	55

3. Descriptive Writing · 63
    Words to describe emotions · 66
    Describing physical characteristics · 67
    Using figurative language in descriptive writing · 68
    Organising the description · 69
    Be specific · 72

4. Summary · 77
    Generalising examples · 80
    Taking notes and underlining · 88

5. Reports · 99
    Format · 102

About the Author · 109

Preface

Most other textbooks for English A focus on comprehension and grammar exercises. Writing Workshop satisfies the need for a text to fill the gap in relation to development of skills needed to write summaries, speeches ,arguments and other forms of persuasive writing, short stories, reports and descriptions.

Writing Workshop is directed at high school students, adults pursuing additional qualifications and taking classes or engaging in self- directed study in order to pass CXC English A examinations or improve their writing skills for work.

The text includes numerous activities for practice as well as samples of writing to provide a guide to the appropriate skill level expected.

It is a highly valuable instructional text for teachers, those in the tutoring business and for parents assisting their children to improve their writing skills.

1

Persuasive Writing

Getting Started

If you like to argue about sports, your favourite team and player or if you sometimes have a heated discussion with your friends about which basketball team is better then you have used persuasive language and techniques to express your point of view. You are probably quite emotional in these discussions and sometimes even illogical. That may be excusable in these informal situations but in situations where you want to be taken seriously you need to have a sound argument. Here are some techniques to help you to write or speak persuasively. Let us start with writing persuasively.

Your task or assignment usually requires you to write an essay or an article. It allows you to choose a point of view, to disagree or agree with a particular statement. You are really setting out to show that your opinion is absolutely the right one.

Here is a sample topic. **Schools should institute random searches of students' backpacks to check for illegal weapons. Do you agree?**

Now follow these steps.

1. Choose a side or point of view.

2. Collect points or reasons to support your opinion or stance.

3. Have at least three points or reasons to support your argument. You can aim for a total of four or five points. You cannot make a convincing argument with less than three points.

4. Switch to the other point of view if you cannot find enough points to support your argument. There is no rule that says that you have to choose the side that you like better. Your personal beliefs are important but if you have no support for them you cannot create a convincing argument. Try collecting points to support the other side of the argument.

5. Review your points and organize them in order of strength. The strongest point will be your first point. You can put numbers beside the points to show the order in which you will use them.

6. Develop and support each point. You can use examples, illustrations, statistics, references to authorities, and quotations from experts and trusted sources.

7. Develop one point in each paragraph. Try to move smoothly from one paragraph to another, using connectives.

8. Use persuasive techniques such as exaggeration for emphasis, repetition of a phrase or structure also for emphasis, rhetorical questions, emotive language, anecdotes and figurative language.

9. Always begin your argument with a strong statement which leaves no doubt about your opinion. End by reinforcing this stance but naturally you should not use the same words.

10. At some point in the argument you can refer to a point you expect will be raised in opposition to your argument. Refute this point.

> 📁 **authorities:**
>
> sources whether persons, institutions, organisations or publications with extensive knowledge or information on a topic.
>
> A psychologist who has written extensively on juvenile delinquency would be an authority on the subject.

Fig. 1.1 Summary of main steps in constructing a piece of persuasive writing.

Be logical
- Collect points
- At least three

Arrange
- Organise points in order of strength

Expand
- Develop points.
- One point per paragraph

Return to the sample topic. **Schools should institute random searches of students' backpacks to check for illegal weapons. Do you agree?**

Now follow the steps outlined earlier and summarised in the chart above.

Choose a point of view. Let us agree in the first place.

4 | WRITING WORKSHOP

AGREE

Now gather reasons for agreeing. Some possible reasons are

1. Reduction of the violence in schools
2. Reduction of the threat of serious injury
3. Students will feel safer
4. Increased confidence of students in the school's administration
5. Improvement in the learning environment

DISAGREE

Now let us switch to the other point of view. Here are some possible points.

1. Searches will invade the privacy of the students.
2. Searches can cause confrontations between students and administrative officials.
3. Searches are ineffective.

Choose to write on the point of view for which you have more reasons or support. Your persuasive writing will be stronger.

Logic and reason

Your points should be logical and reasonable. It would not be logical to support your disagreement by saying:-

1. Students are old enough to bring weapons to school.

2. Students are not likely to use the weapons they bring to school.

Always give logical, credible reasons to support your point of view.

Prioritise

Now organise and prioritise the points putting the strongest first, then the second strongest and so on until the weakest is the last point.

Use the points which were given in support of the sample topic. Your priority list of those points will look like this.

Table 1.1 Organising the points.

PRIORITY	POINT
FIRST	It will reduce violence in schools.
SECOND	Students will feel safer.
THIRD	It will reduce the threat of serious injury.
FOURTH	It will improve the learning environment.
FIFTH	It will increase the students' confidence in the administration.

Beginning with the strongest point will help you capture the attention of the reader immediately.

Have a strong introduction. Refer to the present problem in schools which would lead to searches. Indicate that searches are an effective way of stemming the flow of illegal weapons onto school campuses.

Here is another sample topic.

Students should not be allowed to use cell phones in the classroom. Write an essay either supporting or opposing this view.

Look at the list of points which support the view and those which oppose it.

Arrange the points in order of strength putting strongest points first. Begin with the supporting list and then arrange the opposing list.

Fig. 1.2 List of points prioritised

SUPPORT
- Students can use cell phones for cheating
- Cell phones distract students from learning
- Use of phones reduces teaching time and undermines effective classroom control
- Students lack maturity to use phones appropriately
- Cell phones can lead to confrontations in the classroom

OPPOSE
- cell phones can be used as teaching tools
- students can use use phones as reference and resource aids
- phones may become necessary for emergency contact

Developing a paragraph

The list of points will not make an argument or essay. You must develop each point into a paragraph of at least four or five sentences.

Practise building or developing a paragraph. Begin the paragraph with the point you want to make. That will be the topic sentence. Imagine that the sentence below is your topic sentence.

> *The use of cell phones in the classroom can encourage cheating.*

Use the following questions to help you build your paragraph.

Who?

What?

Why?

How?

Where?

When?

The most logical question arising from the topic sentence is "How?" Let us answer that question. You can do that by giving an example of the way a cell phone can be used for cheating.

> **EXAMPLE**
> *During a test or examination a student can use a cell phone to contact someone on the outside or another student in the room for assistance with the answers. This can happen quite easily because cell phones can quietly and quickly convey text messages.*

Use another example to strengthen the case you are making. This will help to illustrate more clearly and give support to the topic sentence.

> **EXAMPLE 2**
> *It is also possible for a student who has a smart phone like a BlackBerry to use it to search the internet for information during an examination.*

Look at the questions again and the next most logical question is "What?". You can answer that by giving the consequences of the examples.

> **CONSEQUENCE**
> *Using the cell phone in this way will give a student an unfair advantage over his other classmates.*

Conclusion. You can conclude the paragraph with a persuasive device. In this case you can use a rhetorical question.

> **PERSUASIVE DEVICE – RHETORICAL QUESTION**
> *Why give a student an easy opportunity to cheat?*
>
> *These are strong reasons to ban students from using cell phones in the classroom.*

Here is another example of paragraph development. Follow and identify the stages of development.

Imagine that you have to convince the education authorities to keep the physical education programme which is threatened by reductions in public spending.

TOPIC SENTENCE
Physical education will improve the health of students.

WHY?

Students today are less active than their counterparts of fifteen years ago. Many are not participating in actual sporting activities, preferring to play video games instead.

WHAT is the consequence?

As a result, many teenagers, and children as young as eight years old are obese and are developing illnesses such as diabetes.

Go back to the topic sentence and ask another question. HOW?

Physical education in the schools may be the only opportunity for many students to get some exercise. The games, swims and hikes of the classes keep students moving and in that way they obtain the healthful benefits of exercise.

ADDITIONAL SUPPORT:
Reference to an authority on the matter. Use of statistics.

A recent study by the Caribbean Health Institute found that schools with a physical education programme had thirty percent fewer obese students than those schools which had no such programme.

>  Now find two other points in support of retaining the physical education programme in schools and construct and develop a paragraph for each point.
>
> - Begin with the point you want to make as your topic sentence.
>
> - Give an explanation of the point in one or two sentences.
>
> - Provide an example or illustration to support your point.
>
> - Use one of the persuasive techniques to give emphasis to your point.

Use this same pattern for other paragraphs but vary the type of support you use. In one paragraph refer to an authority such as a book or an article by an expert whose opinions match yours.

In another paragraph you can refer to statistics to support your point of view. Use another persuasive technique. Try repeating a phrase for emphasis.

Build each paragraph in this way.

Now construct your conclusion. End by repeating your original position in new words of course. Express yourself emphatically.

Getting the flow

Let your paragraphs flow smoothly from one to another. Use linking words such as: 'in addition', 'secondly', 'another reason', 'along with'.

You can also put related points in paragraphs that are close together to give more unity and coherence to the writing.

In Table 1.2 are some examples of linking words.

Table 1.2 Examples of linking words.

Linking words		
similarly	in the same way	as a result
consequently	therefore	besides
however	another	despite
additionally	accordingly	finally

Suggestions for openings

You should always try to have an arresting or interesting opening for your persuasive writing. Here are some suggestions for beginning your persuasive essay or argument:

- a quotation
- an assertive personal declaration of your opposition or agreement
- reference to a statistic which supports your point of view
- a fact that illustrates your point of view
- a provocative rhetorical question
- an anecdote

Let us look at the following topic.

A country that chooses agriculture for its main economic activity will remain undeveloped. Give your views.

Here are samples of each suggested type of openings.

interesting fact

In the 17th century when the epic Industrial Revolution transformed the United Kingdom from an agricultural to an industrialised nation it initiated the process that brought progress and development to Great Britain.

rhetorical question

After 300 years of dependence on sugar cane and banana cultivation can any of the Caribbean countries be considered rich?

statistics

Wheat sells for US$280 per ton while the price of steel is US$857 per ton. Agriculture is a low income earner but manufacture is a high income earner.

anecdote

My grandfather worked hard at his farm in the mountains day after day. Food was always on the table but there was little of anything else. His family lived in a wooden shack and when he died he owned nothing not even the land which he had farmed.

quotation

"Agriculture not only gives riches to a nation but the only riches she can call her own." Samuel Johnson was right then and he is still right even today.

assertive personal declaration

Man cannot exist without food. This is a permanent demand that must be satisfied. A well-managed sustainable and commercial agricultural sector can lead to a country's economic development.

Persuasive Writing

Activity 1.1

1. Read the statements below. Make two lists for each statement – one of points supporting, the other of points opposing the statement.

    a) Each list should have five points.

    b) Prioritise each list according to the strength of the points.

    c. Begin with the strongest point first.

Statement One

It is better to drop out of school and start a business than to go to university.

Statement Two

Alternative energy is not reliable. Nothing works but oil.

Statement Three

Developed countries should be the ones responsible for eliminating climate change.

2. Develop the paragraphs below using about 100 words. Use the following tips to assist you.

    a) *A part time job helps a teenager to become accustomed to the level of authority in a workplace. It is especially important for a teenager to become exposed to the authority of a boss or supervisor on the job.* ....

- Answer the question, "Why" in order to write sentence three.

- Contrast the authority of the workplace with the authority usually experienced by a teenager.

- Use an anecdote for illustration

    a) *The limited portability of landline telephones is contributing to their declining use.*

    - How?
    - Why is portability important? Who finds it especially important?
    - Use statistics
    - Quote an authority
    - Include a persuasive device

    b) *Text messaging and typing shortcuts on email are reducing students' ability to write Standard English.*

    - What is the problem?
    - Give an example
    - A quotation from an expert, a teacher or a student
    - Statistics or results of research

    c) *A career in professional sports is a means of escaping poverty.*

    - How?
    - Statistics to show average earnings in professional sports
    - An anecdote for illustration
    - Use a persuasive device – rhetorical question

Sample persuasive writing

The following sample of persuasive writing based on the topic given at the beginning of the chapter, is partially completed. Read the sample then follow the instructions below it.

Schools should institute random searches of students' backpacks to check for illegal weapons. Do you agree?

There is too much violence in the schools. Principal Fahie is quite right to introduce the random search of backpacks for illegal weapons. I firmly believe that it will reduce the violence on campus. Students are not afraid to bring weapons to school because they know they will not be caught. They are less likely to bring a weapon to school if their bags will be searched especially as they will not know when searches will be conducted. Few students would want to be caught with a weapon in their bags. When students have fewer weapons to resort to there will be less fights because the weapons make the students feel bold enough to start and participate in fights.

 Students will feel safer in school if the random searches take place. A recent survey by the local police found that persons indicated that they felt safer at a function when the patrons are searched on entry. Students will feel the same sense of security when they see weapons being taken away and will realize that the searches discourage the bringing of weapons to school. Fewer weapons will mean a safer school because the weapons encourage violence. Why take the chance of bloodshed in the school when there is such a quick and simple solution?

The searches may even save a life, for fewer students will be exposed to the threat of serious injury. Fistfights between students are far less likely to result in severe injury but weapons mean instant injury including stabbings, lacerations and deep cuts. It is better to search the backpacks and stop the bloodshed. Just last week, The Daily Mirror reported that shots were fired from inside a school bus. Students from one school were shooting at others from another school. The police found the gun in the backpack of a female student right among the papers and other school materials. A search at school would have discovered the weapon. It was pure luck that no one was seriously hurt or worse.

Teachers would accomplish more during class time.

Complete the third paragraph. Use the steps given earlier for developing a paragraph. Use repetition for emphasis and use statistics to help support your point.

> **Principal Fahie is my hero for instituting the strong response of searching the back packs.**

The above sentence is the final sentence of the concluding paragraph. Write the concluding paragraph ending with the above sentence.

Letters to the Editor

Writing a letter to the editor of a newspaper is one way of expressing your opinion on a particular issue. It is another example of persuasive writing. You want to get all the readers of the newspaper to agree with your point of view. You will employ all the basic techniques for persuasive writing. The letter will be shorter than an article on the same topic. You will also use a more direct and informal tone. You can make more use of the persuasive techniques such as the rhetorical question, figurative language and sarcasm sometimes. You can also employ exaggeration and repetition for emphasis. Try appealing to the emotions.

Here are some examples. Identify the points the writer makes. Identify the persuasive techniques. In Sample Letter 1 the writer wants garbage bins returned to the city streets.

Sample letter to the Editor 1

Dear Editor

I am so ashamed at the piles of litter on our city's streets. Food containers, soda and water bottles roll around on the streets while empty snack packages lie trapped against fences and railings. The truth is that the streets have become huge garbage bins.

I agree that many of our citizens are careless about where they dispose of their litter. But can you blame them? Take a good look up and down our city streets and you will not find a garbage bin in sight. Years ago you could find a garbage bin at convenient intervals along the streets. Most people would drop in their empty food packets, gum wrappers and soda bottles as they passed. Then the Solid Waste Management Department had the very bright idea to remove the bins because in the department's expert opinion they made the city untidy. "Take your garbage home with you," they said.

Did they really expect ladies to put their soiled and dirty food wrappers in their handbags to take them home? Or should we put the empty water bottles in our pockets until we get home? It is totally unrealistic. Who would carry garbage around with them all day? Well I am sure that they can see that nobody takes home garbage and the city is more untidy now. What was overflowing from the bins is now overflowing on the streets.

I would not be surprised if there is an outbreak of disease in the city as the rodents and flies enjoy the squalor.

I wonder what visitors think when they leave their luxury cruise ship only to be confronted by a dirty mess. I am surprised that they still come to our shores.

If anyone cares to join me I will be marching down to South Lane outside the headquarters of the Solid Waste Management

Department. Let us hold hands and chant, "Put back the bins! Put back the bins!"

*Yours sincerely
Mary Cleanstreet*

The letter to the Editor is persuading the relevant authorities to keep the streets clean. A letter to the editor is briefer than an essay or article. Fewer reasons are supplied. There is more use of persuasive devices.

The chart below identifies the reasons and persuasive devices used by the writer in the sample letter.

Fig 1.3 List of reasons and persuasive devices in Sample Letter to the Editor 1

Reasons
- Failure of no bin policy
- Threat to public health
- Threat to tourism industry

Persuasive devices
- Exaggeration

  Streets have become huge garbage bins

- Sarcasm

  bright idea

- Rhetorical questions

  Who would carry garbage around with them all day?

- Appeal to emotion

  rodents and flies enjoy the squalor

Sample Letter to the Editor 2

Dear Editor

I know that most people believe that teenagers do not read, but some of us still do. I am sorry to say though, that our Public Library does not encourage the reading habit. I have not found even five new titles in the teenage collection for as many years. I am sure that authors are still producing good books but our Public Library does not seem to know this. The collection is so stagnant that the books are greeting me like old friends.

What makes it more discouraging for a young reader like me is the deplorable condition of the few available titles. Covers are falling off and some pages are even missing. The workers seem content to let the books fall apart. My parents tell me that in their day the Public Library used to repair and bind the shabby books. Well, clearly, that is an old habit that has died.

How can adults complain that teenagers do not read enough when the Public Library itself does more to discourage than encourage young people to read?

I was also wondering who determined the opening hours. Last Saturday morning I settled in at midday to work on a history assignment. I had barely started when they began to turn off the lights. I learned to my dismay that the library closes at 1:00 p.m. on Saturdays. How can the Public Library close early on the day that students have the most time to spend there?

I call on those in authority to realize the importance of the Public Library and make some changes to encourage young people to use the facility. Take action soon or you will lose all teenagers to the video games.

Yours sincerely
Frustrated teen reader

Letters to the editor often include a call to action. Both sample letters end with a call to action.

WRITING WORKSHOP

> Write for your audience.
>
> Determine your audience.
>
> An audience is the target of your writing.
>
> Your vocabulary and tone should be appropriate for your audience or you will lose their attention.
>
> Notice that the tone of the letters to the editor differs from that of the speech by President Obama.

Activity 1.3

1. Make your own list of the reasons that the writer of the second sample letter gives to persuade the authorities to make changes. Identify the persuasive devices used in the letter.

2. An article in the local newspaper has suggested a 7:00 p.m. curfew for all teenagers in order to reduce crime. Write a letter to the editor of the newspaper either agreeing with the suggestion or opposing it.

3. Write a letter to the editor of the local newspaper giving your opinion of the government's plan to provide each high school student with a laptop computer.

4. Some parents have written to the local newspaper criticising the practice of holding elaborate and expensive high school graduation ceremonies and parties. Write a letter to the editor of the newspaper either supporting the parents or disagreeing with them.

5. The youths of your area use the community sports facilities on a daily basis. Write a letter to the Editor of a local newspaper commending the authorities for providing these facilities in your community.

WRITING TIPS

Have bright, clear ideas.

Brainstorm. Write your ideas as they come to you.

Have logical points.

Search for sources of information to get ideas.

Use the library, the internet, parents and teachers. Try these sites: www.unesco.org, www.fao.org, www.undp.org. You will find information on science, agriculture and global population.

Go to www.ted.com for talks and videos on a variety of topics.

Speech

The same procedures of persuasive writing apply if you are preparing a persuasive speech. The tone and content of your speech will depend on your audience. Your audience can be your classmates, parents, church leaders, the Chamber of Industry and Commerce. It can be members of your community. Write as if speaking to an audience. Refer to your audience during the speech e.g. "parents", "classmates", "musicians".

You still need to gather and determine the points you will make. You still need to make one point at a time and to develop the point. Because a speech needs to keep the interest of an audience you should include more persuasive techniques than you would include in an essay. Rhetorical questions work very well in a speech. So does repetition. The tone of a speech will differ from that of an article or essay. The tone of the speech will be more personal and direct as the speaker tries to engage his audience.

Make appeals to feelings and qualities to which your audience can relate. You can appeal to their desire to be prosperous, their love of country or their loyalty to school and community. These are just examples. Your appeals will depend on the purpose of the speech and the audience.

The following are pointers to note when preparing a speech.

Be mindful of audience
- make message appropriate to audience
- address and include audience

Use persuasive devices
- rhetorical questions
- repetition
- exaggeration for emphasis

Make emotional appeals
- love of community
- need for safety
- care of family

Use appropriate tone
- for occasion
- for audience

Examine this excerpt from the victory speech of US President Barack Obama. The speech was delivered after he won the presidential elections of the United States in 2008.

"If there is anyone out there who still doubts that America is a place where all things are possible; who still wonders if the dream of our founders is alive in our time; who still questions the power of our democracy, tonight is your answer.

It's the answer told by lines that stretched around schools and churches in numbers this nation has never seen; by people who waited three hours and four hours, many for the very first time in their lives, because they believed that this time must be different; that their voices could be that difference.

It's the answer spoken by young and old, rich and poor, Democrat and Republican, black, white, Hispanic, Asian, Native American, gay, straight, disabled and not disabled - Americans who sent a message to the world that we have never been just a collection of individuals or a collection of Red States and Blue States: we are, and always will be, the United States of America.

It's the answer that led those who have been told for so long by so many to be cynical, and fearful, and doubtful of what we can achieve to put their hands on the arc of history and bend it once more toward the hope of a better day.

It's been a long time coming, but tonight, because of what we did on this day, in this election, at this defining moment, change has come to America."

In the first paragraph the sections highlighted in **orange** show the speaker's engagement with the audience. The repetition of the word "our' in paragraph one and the use of the word "we" throughout the speech are also other ways of engaging the audience.

The sections in the speech highlighted in **pink** show the use of repetition as a device to hold the attention of the audience. It emphasizes the point the speaker is making and attempts to persuade the audience to the speaker's point of view.

The speaker appeals to the listeners'

pride in their country - "we are, and always will be, the United States of America."

desire to be considered important and their desire to be a part of an important event - "to put their hands on the arc of history and bend it"

Below is another example of a speech.

Sample speech

Speech to members of a community to encourage the residents to restore their old schoolroom.

> *Residents of Moon Hill, what does that crumbling structure on the hill mean to you? To our parents it was the place where they learned to read and write; the first of their families to have that opportunity. It was the place where they learnt to hope for a life beyond the canefields and cotton fields. Should such a place be left neglected and rundown as if it had no meaning and importance?*
>
> *Let us give the old schoolhouse a makeover that suits its position in the history of our community.*
>
> *The old schoolhouse laid the foundation for the prosperity that our community enjoys today. It is from that simple school house that our engineers, lawyers and doctors sprang. It is from that*

schoolhouse our farmers and fishermen have come. It is from that schoolhouse come the men that build our houses. We owe so many of our achievements as a community to the lessons that were taught and learnt in the old schoolhouse.

As a young nation we have so few monuments. It is time that we begin to preserve the symbols that preserve our history. We can start here in Moon Hill with our own simple monument. Instead of letting the schoolroom crumble and decay into the dust, we can work together to restore and rebuild one of the things that built us and our community.

What we do with the schoolhouse will show what type of citizens we are. Be grateful and right thinking citizens. Restore the old schoolhouse and you will build for the present and the future generations of Moon Hill residents, a symbol of pride and achievement.

The speaker makes several appeals.

He appeals to:

- the pride of the residents.
- the desire to make a difference in the community
- the nostalgia of the residents
- the desire to leave a legacy behind
- a sense of responsibility

He uses:

- rhetorical questions
- repetition

26 | WRITING WORKSHOP

Using the sample speech above:-

1. Identify the main points made.
2. Underline the examples of rhetorical questions and repetition.
3. Quote the words and phrases that make the different appeals.
4. Identify the audience.

Activity 1.4

1. Your high school plans to stage a "Television- free Week" during which all students will forego watching television from Monday to Friday of one week. Prepare the speech you as president of the student council will make to the parent teachers association to persuade parents to participate in the event along with the students.

2. Imagine you are the president of the student council. Prepare the speech you would make to persuade fifth form students to volunteer at the local community outreach centre which provides meals for the homeless and for needy persons.

Figure 1.4 lists several useful steps to assist you with preparing this speech. Read the list and note and apply the suggestions.

Fig.1.4 Tips for creating a speech.

> **Find at least three reasons for volunteering**
> - make the reasons relevant for the audience
> - develop the points or reasons

> **Choose the appeals to make to the audience**
> - be mindful of the age of the audience
> - think of the interests of the audience

> **Use persuasive devices**
> - try at least two rhetorical questions
> - repeat a phrase at the beginning of three consecutive sentences

3. A coastal village in your country is often severely affected by storm surge during hurricanes and tropical storms. The residents are resisting the relocation of the community. Imagine that you are a community leader. Prepare a speech that you will give to persuade the residents to move.

    a) Find three reasons to support the move.

    b) Use the following appeals
       - safety of the community
       - fear
       - financial prudence
       - protection of the young and old

WRITING WORKSHOP

    c) Include three consecutive sentences each beginning with the words, "How much longer" in one of the paragraphs.

4. The proposed noise abatement legislation will require that parties in residential areas end at 2:00 a.m. The authorities are holding a town hall meeting in your area to discuss the legislation with residents. Make a speech at the meeting either supporting or opposing the proposed time for cessation of parties.

5. Practise the following persuasive writing exercises.

Persuasive writing practice exercises

1. Governments in the region should ban imported food. Either support or disagree with the statement.
2. There should be no compulsory subjects on the high school curriculum. Do you agree?
3. Oil is the only reliable energy source. Alternative energy is not reliable. Write an essay either supporting or refuting the argument.
4. Your high school has organized a student exchange program with a high school in Puerto Rico in order to help students improve their fluency in Spanish. Prepare a speech to be delivered to the Parent Teachers Association to gain support for the programme
5. All citizens should pay taxes. Write an article supporting this statement.
6. High school students do not need a guidance counsellor. Write an article for the school magazine opposing this point of view.
7. The organisers of a club of fourteen year old boys have invited you to address the group on the dangers of joining a gang. Write the speech you will make.
8. Write a letter to the editor of the local newspaper supporting or opposing the opening of a dolphin attraction for tourists.
9. Speaker A: There is no such thing as global warming.
   Speaker B: Melting glaciers tell a different story.
   Write an essay supporting the views of either Speaker A or Speaker B.

📁 Resources

- Use the following resources to obtain information and ideas for your persuasive writing.

newspapers and magazines	radio and television programmes
panel discussions and debates	online articles
speeches	websites

- Keep abreast of issues often debated including

local and international current events	sports
social issues	cultural changes
business and economics	environment

2
Short Story

Elements

A short story is fiction. It is created by the writer. It consists of an event or a series of events in which one or more individuals are involved. The action usually builds to a high point very quickly. A short story has several basic elements.

- Plot
- Setting
- Character
- Dialogue
- Conflict

Plot

The **plot** is the storyline or plan of what will happen in the story. It is the foundation or blue print of the story. When you decide on a plot then you know how your story will begin, progress and conclude. Just think of some of the children's television cartoons you watch or you used to watch.

A cartoon's basic plot is that a major character will try to achieve a goal and another character will do everything to prevent it. The good character usually wins in the end. If the bad character is the one setting out to do something awful then the good character will do everything to prevent him. This is the example of a basic plot.

To make the plot complete you decide what the characters intend to do and how they intend to achieve their individual goals.

If Evil Tonka wants to take over the world how will he do this? Will he use bombs? Will he turn the adults to stone? Will he get all the animals on his side?

> *Evil Tonka wants to take over the world.*
>
> *He freezes all the water.*
>
> *Super Vendi sets out to stop him.*
>
> *Evil Tonka traps him and freezes him in a block of ice.*
>
> *Super Vendi uses his super breath to escape.*
>
> *He searches for Tonka's headquarters and destroys the freezing machine.*

The **resolution** of the story is the way the plot ends. The resolution can be expected or it can be surprising.

See the simple plot in sidebar.

Setting

The **setting** of a story is the location of the story in time and place. Your story can be set in a household, in a rural or urban area. It can take place in the past, in the future or in the present, on a ship or in a cave. There are lots of interesting possibilities.

Associated with the setting is the **atmosphere** of the story. Do you want it to be gloomy and forbidding or gay and exciting? It can change within the story. The atmosphere will reflect the actions and moods of the characters.

Characters

The **characters** are the people in the story. Give them names, physical characteristics and personalities. Suggest their ages. Make them interact. Animals can also be characters. In Herman Melville's *Moby Dick* the white whale is a character, with a name and a personality.

You can give an indication of the personality of the character through his or her words and actions.

> *Tonka's face twisted in a sly smile as he watched the bunch of noisy boys hurrying along to the pool for a midday swim. He twisted the dial on his wrist Freezemator.*
>
> *"That ought to cool them down fast. Minus 40 degrees. Don't have to watch. I'll just listen to the screams."*

Tonka's smile, his action of turning down the temperature of the pool, and his words showing anticipated delight in the boys' pain are used to create a mean sadistic character.

Dialogue

Characters in a story will speak to other characters or even to themselves. This is **dialogue** – the conversation of characters, the actual words of the characters as they speak.

Use dialogue to further the action of the story and to give life to your characters. Do not include dialogue merely for the sake of having dialogue.

> *"When I get you Tonka, I'll turn your own Freezemator on you!" shouted Super Vendi.*
>
> *"Your brain is too small to figure out how to get me," taunted Tonka.*

Do not include it merely to complete the checklist of components of a story. The dialogue must form an integral part of the story. Your characters can whisper to one another in a dangerous or scary situation. That is dialogue. They can be warning one another or encouraging or even disagreeing about an action or a person. Your plot will determine what conversations will take place, what shouts will be heard, what communication will take place. You should use quotation marks when writing dialogue.

Conflict

A story's basis is **conflict.** A conflict is a struggle. The conflict may be between characters as between Tonka and Super Vendi in the simple plot outlined earlier. The struggle can be against an organization, a business, even an animal or a force of nature. A farmer may struggle against the effects of a drought. The conflict could also be internal. A character may struggle with himself over making a decision. He may struggle against a weakness, a fear or a bad habit.

The conflict is often the reason or the force behind the actions of the characters. A character may overcome her fear or she may surrender to her fear.

When a character ends the struggle there is **resolution** of the conflict.

Storyline

The story line gives the time path of the story. The most common story line is chronological. The story moves forward as time itself moves. You can however begin a story in the present and then continue it by going back to the past. This is called a flashback technique. Choose the storyline that you feel most competent to handle.

Short Story | 35

Fig 2.1 Chronological and flashback storylines

| chronological today | → | always moving tomorrow | → | forward next week |

⬆ **Flashback.**
Going forward

⬇ **then remembering and reliving the past**

Sample flashback opening.

> *Karen stepped down the aisle on the arm of her father. She glanced at his clean-shaven profile. She heard the organ play the "Wedding March". The day was perfect. Flowers along the aisle and on the church columns wafted their fragrance towards her. She still could hardly believe it but she could not forget the day her luck had changed.*
>
> *The flight was full. It was the last available seat on the plane. She pushed her way to the back wearily.*
>
> *"Can I just squeeze past you?"*
>
> *The old man in the aisle seat was already nodding off. He blinked up at her.*

Here the story begins on the wedding day and continues in the present up to the words, "luck had changed."

The flashback to the past begins at, "The flight was full." Such a story will continue to relate past events that led to the wedding.

The Narrator

The narrator is the person who is telling the story. You can use a third person narrator. This is someone who is seeing everything and knows what the other characters are thinking, feeling and doing. This is the type of narrator which is most often used.

You can also have a first person narrator. This means that one of the characters in the story is telling the story.

"I watched as my last match disappeared." This suggests that the "I" would tell the story.

The narrator can be of any age or gender. You may be a seventeen year old girl but you can write your story from any point of view. You can write as a boy, as a man, as a six year old, an older woman, even as an animal, a house or a boat.

Write one paragraph of a story from each of the following points of view.

1. A turtle returning to the beach to lay eggs.

"The way home was long. I had left the sea grass beds of the Mediterranean."

2. The thirteen year old class bully.

   "His nose was bloody and he crawled away from me."

3. An alien who witnesses the first moon landing

4. A boy finds an old trunk stored in a shed. Let the trunk begin to tell its story.

Working With The Elements

Creating a character

When creating a character **show** the reader what the character is like rather than **tell** the reader.

> **Example:**
>
> **Tell -** Joe is a hardworking fisherman.
>
> **Show -** Joe untied his boat in the grey light of dawn. Only two other boats were already out on the water. He stowed his torch and his windbreaker on board. He knew he would need them. By the time he came back the sun would be down and there would be a little nip in the air.

You can show what the character is like by

- putting the person in a situation and describing his actions and reactions.
- using his words, his conversations
- showing how others behave towards him or around him
- recording his thoughts

Create a character who is a fisherman in an urban area.

Here are some helpful guidelines.

1. What is his stature or his gait?

2. What is his name?

3. What is he wearing?

4. Describe the features of his face, his skin and his eyes.

5. What is he like as a person? How would you show that?

6. Describe his eyes so that they give a clue to his character.

7. Do the same with his hands.

Dialogue

You must make your dialogue realistic and appropriate to the characters. Let your teenaged characters speak as teenagers would, parents as parents and striking workers as striking workers would. Use dialect where it fits the characters and the action.

Make your dialogue appropriate to the action or situation or the emotion of the moment. Dialogue can show anxiety, excitement, anger or fear, in fact any emotion. In this way it would help to create the atmosphere you want. Here is an example.

Fig 2.3 Dialogue showing emotion and creating atmosphere.

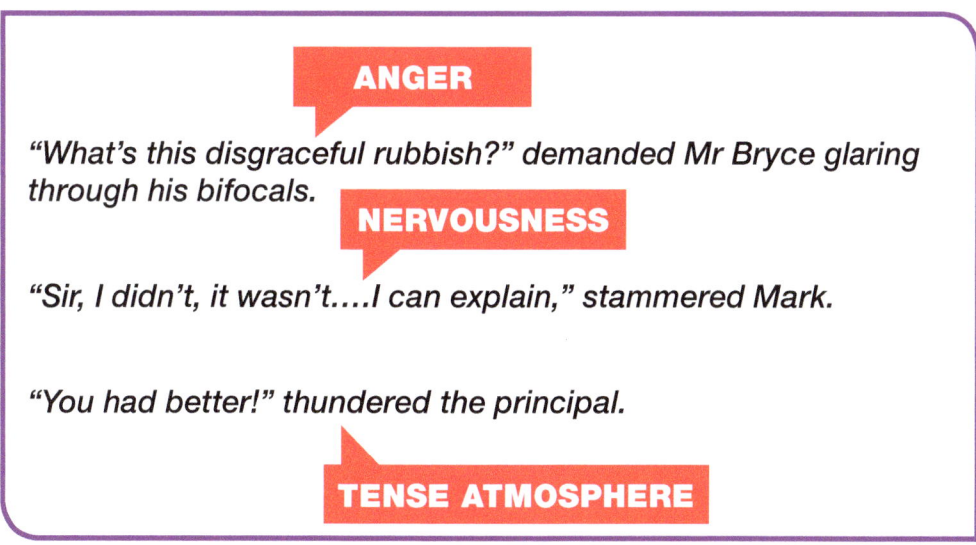

Remember that the dialogue also helps you to portray the personality of the characters.

You can get ideas for dialogue by listening. Conversations and exchanges are always happening around you. Pay attention! How does the street vendor talk to a customer? What is the conversation like in the barbershop? How do little boys and girls talk to their friends?

Punctuate dialogue properly. Use quotation marks and put each speaker's words on a separate line.

a) Harry has just found a shiny steel cylinder in the grass while crossing a field. There is no opening. It is completely sealed. He hurries to the home of his high school friend Jervan to show him the mysterious object.

Write the dialogue that ensues when they meet. Let each boy speak at least four times.

  b)   In 1930, riots begin on a sugar estate in St Kitts. Eliza, a worker on the estate puts down her tools and hurries to the nearest village.

Write the conversation that takes place between Eliza and the first person she meets. Give that person a name.

Eliza and the other character should have at least four exchanges each.

  c)   Write the conversation between two birds sitting on overhead electricity wires and watching construction work on a house across the street.

  d.   Write the dialogue that takes place between a client and a marketing officer of a manufacturing business. The client wants goods produced and delivered in a short time frame.

Setting

When creating settings you should think of time and place. The times you choose can be in another century whether in the past or in the future. You can set your story in a time ten years ago or fifty years ago. Of course you can also set your story in the present but the past and the future are other choices. The time can also refer to the time of day. The events of your story can take place at dawn or dusk, midday or midnight

Try to create settings which enhance your story. If the first setting that comes to mind is a classroom or your home, try again and think of other locations. Changing the setting may lead to a better plot. Aim for the unusual, for locations that are extraordinary.

Plot

In a short story the action begins immediately and builds to a climax quickly then moves to a resolution.

You can get ideas for plots from books, movies, your travels, sports competitions, other school competitions such as debates and science fairs, and events in the news including international events.

Read the short stories of O Henry and Guy de Maupassant. You will see how these authors move the action along and how they treat a plot.

You can use the usual themes of literature to assist you in shaping a plot for a story.

Some of these themes are:

- heroism
- individual against society
- individual against the environment
- strong principled men/women
- ambition
- individual against his own weakness

Let us suppose that you were given a title **The Turtle Shell** on which to write a story. To help you find a plot you can choose a theme. Preservation of turtles is a popular area of discussion and action. You can place a character against the society. The turtle shell is the evidence of a turtle caught and killed. Your character is defying the rules. Why is he doing this? How will this be resolved? Will he be caught?

You can choose the theme heroism and your main character will find and expose those who are catching the turtles.

The turtle shell can be a symbol. The shell is tough, protective, it belongs to an animal which is known for its longevity, has a strong instinct and is a survivor. The turtle shell can therefore be a logo of a business, a name of a shop or a website that shows the driving force behind the achievement of a goal or a dream. You can tell the story of how the character achieved his dream, how **The Turtle Shell** was born.

You can continue to move away from the literal. **The Turtle Shell** can be an infamous pirate ship of the past. It can be a little pirate boat of the present too. The plot can be the story of a pirate raid on a luxury yacht or oil tanker. It can be the story of the underdog boat named **The Turtle Shell** that wins the annual sailing competition.

Let us **examine the words** in another title for a story - **A narrow escape**.

Escape suggests there is a threat of danger or actual danger. You have to identify the danger.

Escape also means that you were able to free yourself from the danger. Identify how you freed yourself or how you avoided the danger.

"Narrow" means you barely escaped. You almost did not get away.

The diagram in Fig 2.4 shows the brainstorming process.

Fig 2.4 Brainstorming for ideas for a story "A Narrow Escape"

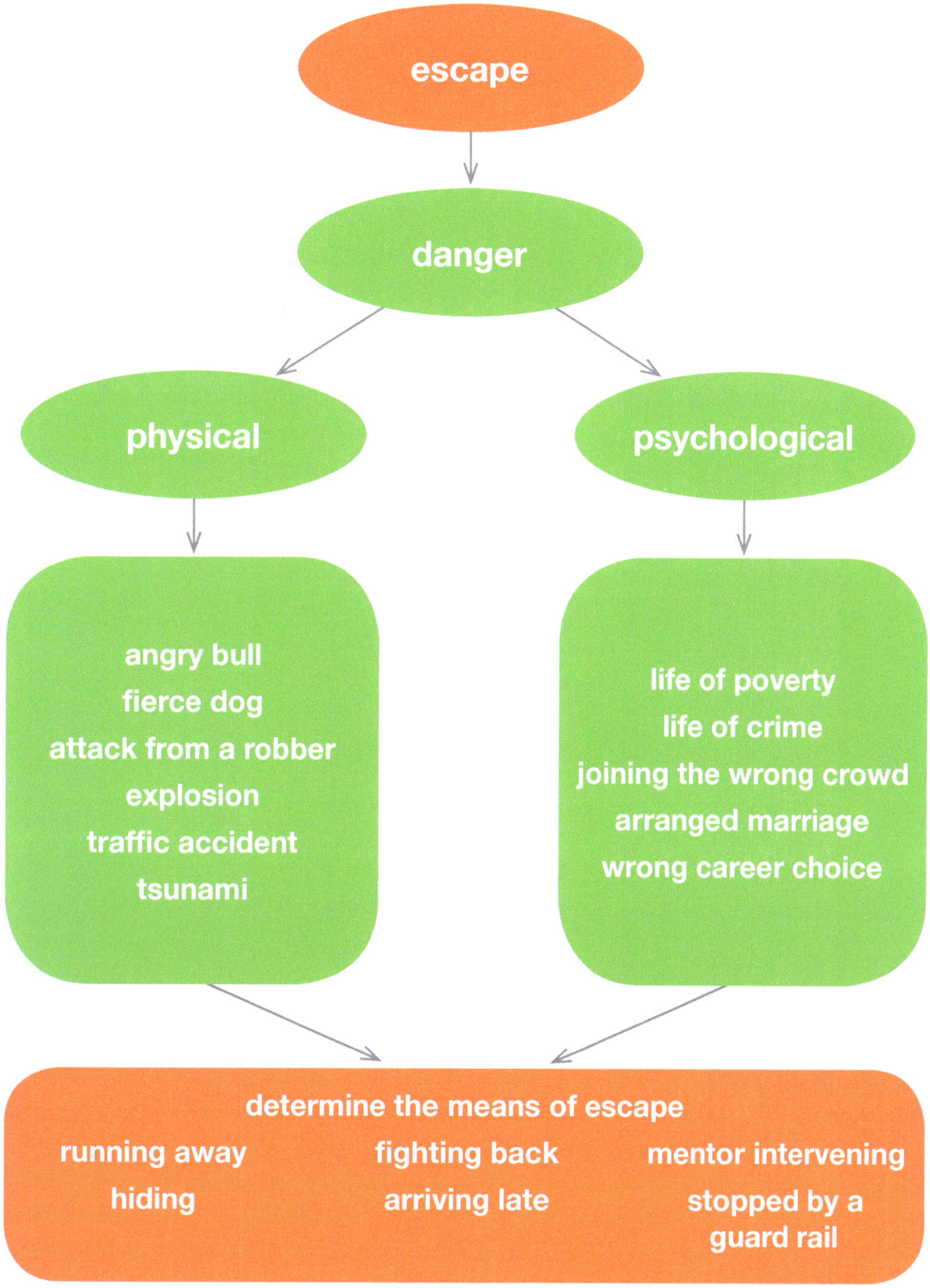

```
                          ┌─────────┐
                          │ escape  │
                          └────┬────┘
                               ▼
                          ┌─────────┐
                          │ danger  │
                          └────┬────┘
                    ┌──────────┴──────────┐
                    ▼                     ▼
              ┌──────────┐         ┌──────────────┐
              │ physical │         │ psychological│
              └─────┬────┘         └───────┬──────┘
                    ▼                      ▼
```

physical:
- angry bull
- fierce dog
- attack from a robber
- explosion
- traffic accident
- tsunami

psychological:
- life of poverty
- life of crime
- joining the wrong crowd
- arranged marriage
- wrong career choice

determine the means of escape

| running away | fighting back | mentor intervening |
| hiding | arriving late | stopped by a guard rail |

44 | WRITING WORKSHOP

Activity 2.3

Create three different settings for a story that includes these words.
"I held my breath and watched as my last remaining matchstick fell out of sight."

Remember a setting can be day or night, urban or rural, desert or wetland, outer space or in a cave. It can be anything that exists on planet earth or in outer space.

Each of the following settings can be used to help create the story around the disappearing last match.

Fig 2.2 Suggested settings

Setting 1
- Cave - wet - slippery
- sound of running water, dogs panting outside

Setting 2
- Crowds - music - smoke rising
- barbecue competition

Setting 3
- Roaring breakers - reef - on a cliff looking out to sea
- midnight

Now move on to build a plot for the story. Choose one of the settings. Ask yourself what circumstances brought you to that setting and situation. What is the problem? Will there be a solution? If there is no solution then determine what will happen. Choose a course of action, create the conflict and determine the result or conclusion of your story.

Below are examples of plots appropriate for each setting.

Setting 1 – plot

Escape from prison, tracked by dogs, hiding in cave, matches to signal rescuer, flashback to crime and trial, plan to escape prison, the struggle to find a way out of the cave, underground river, character crawls and swims in darkness and terror towards light

Setting 2 - plot

Need $10,000 prize to save family home from bank foreclosure. Enter barbecue competition to win the prize. Nervous. Cannot start the fire. Sympathetic competitor gives a burning coal. Uses Uncle Albert's recipe. Fails to win. Despair and dismay. Two weeks later a call from one of the judges – owner of chain of restaurants. Licenses use of recipe. Earns more than enough to save the family home.

Setting 3 – plot

Men go out to smuggle to bring food to starving village. I am assigned the task to light a fire to give smugglers the warning to avoid reefs on their return. I fail to light the fire. The boat is wrecked. I tell no one. The smugglers come home safely the following night. They took another route because of weather. News on the radio – drug smuggling boat wreckage washes up on shore.

Now turn your attention to the characters in the story. Will you have any other characters apart from the narrator? If so how many will you have? What are their names? What personality will each one have? You can give a physical description if it will help your reader to understand the character or even picture the character.

Characters for barbecue competition plot

Some possible characters for this plot are the judges. Give them names such as Chef Cornwall, Mr Osprey and Mrs Teak, and give them physical characteristics and personality traits. Another character would be the friendly competitor who lends the burning coal. Other competitors are likely characters. Some could be jibing and teasing. A good friend who is the only one in whom you confided your intent. A family member, a banker and the master of ceremonies for the competition are all possible characters for the story. You will decide in relation to the way in which you will develop your plot. You the narrator will also be a character in the story. You can be the grandpa or the teenager in the family. You can be male or female.

If you have characters you have to create dialogue. It would be unrealistic to have several characters interacting without speaking at any time. Even if you have no other characters but the narrator, he or she can still talk to the wind, the disappearing match, to himself or herself. But of course this is not necessary. **Here is a short example.**

Dialogue

"What's a boy doing in a man's competition?" Old Chester grumbled into his white beard. "Are you sure you know a barbecue sauce from a soda, boy?"

"Leave him alone Chester. He's got barbecue in his blood," warned Ed the barber, his apron tight around his round belly.

Atmosphere

The environment and the elements of nature can be used to create atmosphere. A bright sunny day and a chatty enthusiastic crowd at the barbecue competition will create a cheerful, hopeful atmosphere. The atmosphere and the setting of the story also help to maintain interest.

You have plot, setting, atmosphere, characters, dialogue now decide on the action put the elements together and write the story.

Practise the same exercise with the other two settings.

Responding to stimulus material

You will receive various forms of stimulus materials from which to create a short story. These are sometimes called story prompts. These could include the following:

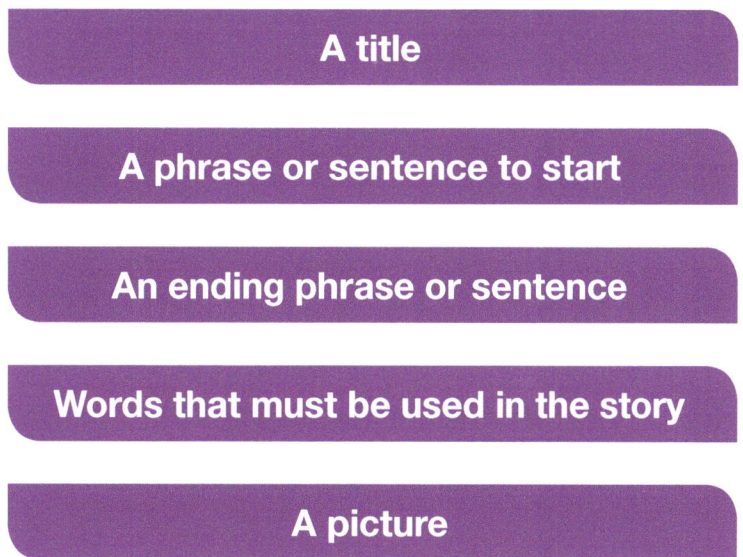

- A title
- A phrase or sentence to start
- An ending phrase or sentence
- Words that must be used in the story
- A picture

A **title** such as **The Turtle Shell** or **The diamond ring** will give you the freedom to use your own words entirely. Just ensure that your plot fits the title even if the Turtle Shell is the name of a boat and even if the diamond ring turns out not to have real diamonds. What is mentioned in the title should be the main focus of the story.

When you are given **words to use in a story** ensure that they fit seamlessly in the story. They should form a natural part of the story and not seem forced into the narrative.

Here is an example using the story prompt given earlier. **He held his breath as he watched his last remaining match fall out of sight.**

> *"Craig groped around for solid footing. It was almost pitch black but he could hear the sound of running water somewhere below him. He felt in his pocket for the matchbox. He took the match out. He bent low trying to block the wind. He felt his foot slipping. He grabbed desperately for a nearby rock. He held his breath as he watched his last remaining match fall out of sight."*

The match is introduced in the story in a way that is natural and easy for the reader to visualize. The character loses his footing and loses the match. This is a very likely incident.

You may be given a sentence or a few sentences with which to start a story, end a story or use anywhere in the story. The following example illustrates the steps you can take to plan such a story.

Let us suppose that you have to start a story with the following sentence. **I grasped the table tightly as the world spun around me.**

1. Determine what parts of the sentence will direct the course of the story. In this case **"as the world spun around me"** is central to the story.

2. Find various interpretations or explanations for that core part of the sentence. In this example you can begin by determining what you mean by the **"world spun around me."** Are you dizzy, fainting anxious, scared, excited or ecstatic?

3. List some events or circumstances that cause the emotion or condition you chose. If for example you chose excitement to explain why **"the world spun around me"** make a list of several scenarios that could lead to such a high level of excitement or happiness. Here are some examples.

   - winning the lottery

   - winning a scholarship

   - hearing a not guilty verdict

4. Choose one of the scenarios and use it to create a plot. What are the events which bring you to a courtroom waiting on a verdict? Why did you play the lottery? Was it out of desperation? Who gave you the scholarship? What did it mean for your future?

5. You can choose a flashback technique for this story if you wish.

6. There is a table in the story. **"I grasped the table tightly"**. This feature is of secondary importance. However you must ensure that you logically place this table in your setting. Do not ignore it.

Let us summarise. When you are given a sentence on which to base a story, you must identify the important parts of that sentence which will give you the basis on which to develop a story.

Here are some examples below.

The shrill screech of the cell phone filled the tiny room. Marlo shut his eyes in dismay.

- Marlo shut his eyes in dismay is the most important part of the prompt. Explanation for his dismay will be a focus point of the plot.

- The description of the cell phone ring as a "shrill screech" makes it seem unpleasant and unwelcome. This will determine the atmosphere of the incident.

- "The tiny room" is a setting that must be determined. That room will help to explain the dismay.

- These three elements are the important clues to begin fashioning a story from the sentences given.

Below are several sentences given to start a story. Identify the elements in each prompt which will be essential in determining the basis of a story.

1. Arnand picked up the crumpled paper and slowly smoothed it out.

2. No one can outdance me Sunil kept telling himself even as he felt the little twinge in his left heel. Undaunted, he kept on walking towards the large squat building.

3. As soon as she held the child in her arms, Maxine knew her life was changed forever.

4. The four white enamelled windmills towered over the pasture like giants. Marcel shielded his eyes and looked up at them with a satisfied smile on his face.

5. Karlene stepped out of the tour bus and slipped on her sunglasses. She could not believe that she was really there.

When you are writing **a story based on a picture**, identify the dominant part or parts of the picture. Let this feature play a role in the story. It could become the setting or help to create the atmosphere. If there are persons in the picture identify the emotions they are expressing or are likely to be expressing. Find a reason for the emotions. This will lead you to a plot.

In this picture the cow is a dominant feature. The cow has a single horn. That is unusual. That single horn can spark the plot for your story. Ask yourself some questions. How did it happen? Who was responsible? Was there a fight with another animal? Will the cow be the main character? Who is the owner? Is he or she as interesting as the cow?

In the background is a ruin. This too can play a part in the story. What is that ruin? Is it the setting of an incident that has become a legend in the village? Is there some superstition surrounding the cow or the ruin?

These and similar questions can help you create a story from the picture.

Openings and closings

Grab the interest of your reader with an arresting opening.

You can start with a conversation or dialogue between two or more characters.

This brings the reader immediately into the action of the story. It introduces the characters immediately and creates curiosity about them and their discussion.

"Let's turn back! It's too wet."

Shhh!" hissed Corpy. "Listen. I heard something."

Another interesting way to begin a story is with a description of a character. The description can be physical or you can describe the personality of the character. Try combining the physical aspects of the person with his personality traits.

Marky was tall, so tall that his mother always had trouble finding shoes to fit his size fifteen feet. He walked with his shoulders bowed a little as if apologizing for his height.

Use a sound to start a story.

Crack! Crack! Crack! The folk dancer's whip flicked the street.

Boom! The sound of thunder reverberated out of the west.

Let the narrator begin by stating his age.

"I am ninety-five now. I was born on Estridge plantation, the year Bas Mills bought the new windmill."

Closing with a twist or surprise ending

You can make a story very memorable and impactful by giving it an ending which is unexpected or surprising. To convey the twist successfully you must maintain the action of the story to make the reader believe or expect the obvious. Build the suspense. Although the end of the story is different from what the reader is expecting, you must make the surprise or twist presented at the end believable and possible in the context of the story.

Here is an example of how you can create a surprise ending.

Let us write a love story. The narrator is sad. Feels like the person he loves has moved on. Describe the loneliness he now experiences. Flash back to the times when they were happy together. They were two professional dancers. Recall the early days, when they were hesitant and unsure of themselves in the world of dance. Move on to the successes, the fame, the travels, the accolades. Build to the peak of their career reflecting the peak of their happiness together. Return to the present. Give subtle hints at the reason for the end of the relationship - new friends, new opportunities and fading looks of the rejected one. Use figurative language to illustrate the despair. Turn the metaphor into the literal. The cast off is revealed as a pair of silken, worn out, tattered, ballet shoes cast off by the star.

To make the ending believable you must emphasise those aspects of a dancer's shoes that are comparable to a loving partner, the love, preference above all others, the beauty, the soft touch, the closeness, anticipation of every move, even the reliability. The story would be an elaborate personification of the ballet shoes.

I watched from the shadows in the corner of the stage as she pirouetted with her new partner.

The sentence above is the first sentence of the final paragraph of the story. Continue the closing paragraph. Make the narrator sad, self-pitying and a little jealous of the one who has taken his place. At the same time let him express his admiration for the star dancer. Move towards the reveal. You can make the narrator himself reveal his identity. You can have the janitor cleaning the stage and removing the shoes with a comment that describes the present condition of the shoes.

Here are some other situations that you can use to create a surprise or twist at the end of a story.

- Let the most trusted character turn out to be the villain.
- A character rescued by the person who seemed most threatening to him.
- A character who celebrates recovery from an addiction was never an addict but an undercover policeman, or a journalist, or a supportive friend.

Avoid using dream endings to create the surprise. This is so overused it is now clichéd. When the dream ending is not well executed it creates a let-down or anti-climax instead of a dramatic finale.

Activity 2.4

Here is a title for a short story. **The Rusty Can.**

Below are three suggestions for creating an opening for the story. Use each suggested method and write three separate opening paragraphs for the story.

- Describe the can in its present location.
- Have the characters express their emotions upon discovery of the can.
- Let the can begin to narrate the story according to the plot you have envisaged.

Sample Short Story

Here is a sample short story.

The Tall Stranger

He came often and always at twilight. The shadowy figure, tall, slightly stooping would wait quietly, shyly and patiently under the neem trees. When her chores were done Aleesa would slip away quietly to join him. Sitting on broad stones under the shelter of the tree, they would talk in hushed tones.

"It is too difficult for a girl to do," she said.

" I know your sense of honour to your family. There will be no shame," he encouraged.

Aleesa stood and walked away a little. She scuffed the earth with her bare toes.

"I need more time. It is too soon…too hard for me to say yet."

"I will come again," he promised. "Together we will overcome your fears."

She watched him leave. His loose robes swirled slightly in the evening breeze. Then he disappeared into the darkness.

Aleesa sat awhile and listened to the sounds of evening. The little village was preparing for night. The woodfires were burning down. Women hurried in with the last jars of water. Their sandals slap, slapped in the quiet. Little puffs of dirt followed on their heels. Sheep baa-ed in their pens.

Aleesa got up slowly. She could hardly bear to enter the dim little house. That night she lay on her pallet curled against the cold. She wondered about life beyond the remote village of poor farmers, dusty roads and hardships.

She rose early as always. Her tight little broom of palm leaf ribs scratched the yard into a neat and clean area. She fetched water from the stream dipping her small gourd and filling her water jar. She lifted the heavy jar on her head balancing it perfectly as she walked.

Later she spooned the thick stew gently and patiently into her Papa's mouth. She cradled his head in the crook of her shoulder raising him so he would not choke. His wasted body always shocked her. She had thought he was invincible, forever strong. He who could follow the plough all day in the burning sun and pull the net full of teeming fish into the slender boat ..now just a shell. The useless legs were shrivelled and bony under the cover. She had woken one morning to find her mother gone. Aleesa never knew whether self- pity or self-preservation had caused her to flee. But she, Aleesa, had stayed for Pap deserved it. She would try to provide for the man who had provided for her.

"Go!" he would say. "You are too young to sacrifice your life for me. Your Aunt Rena will not let me starve."

Aleesa no longer answered him these days. She knew now to hide her anger at his words. She recognised the love behind them. She only patted his head.

"You can't get rid of me, Pap."

She knew too that Aunt Rena would try but hardly had enough for her own family. And who knew when her husband would reject the additional burden of Pap.

"You will just have to stand my cooking."

The little smile he gave cheered her.

He came again. The tall man waited under the trees. It was another full moon. And she was ready. Somehow he knew. He left the package.

She prepared carefully. She washed herself in rosewater from head to toe. She dressed her hair carefully and slid on her arm her slender gold bracelet. The bulk of the package was strangely solid under her clothes. The nearest bus was at least ten miles away. But she felt light and undaunted. As she made her way towards the bus stop, Aleesa knew she was making the right choice. She walked confidently down the dirt road. There would be no turning back.

It was late afternoon when she walked through the bustling market place. She looked around for the tall stranger. For a moment she panicked then she saw him. She nodded. She was ready. Pap would be fine now.

Back in Taban her Aunt Rena wondered at the fat wad of money she had found under the water jar. Where was Aleesa? What had she done?

A month passed before the news of the explosion in the Makeem marketplace reached the remote village. It was a girl this time they said. The martyr was a girl.

Fig. 2.5 Analysing the sample story.

> Does the setting fit the plot?
>
> What does the writer achieve by leaving the stranger unnamed?
>
> What kind of person is Aleesa?
>
> How do you know this?

Pay attention to the use of setting, the characterisation of Aleesa and the tall stranger, even Aleesa's father. Note the way the dialogue adds to the mystery and the characters. Note the ending.

WRITING WORKSHOP

Activity 2.5

Practice exercises

Use the following material to create short stories.

1. When Carol stepped up to receive her prize the whole school shouted and applauded. I sat there quietly. I could not move my hands from my lap.

   Use the questions in Fig. 2.6 below to help you generate ideas for this story.

   Fig. 2.6 Generating ideas.

   > *Answer the following questions to help you shape your story.*
   >
   > *Who is Carol? Why is she getting a prize?*
   >
   > *Why is the reaction of the school so overwhelming?*
   >
   > *Who is the narrator, the "I" of the story?*
   >
   > *Why is the narrator so quiet?*
   >
   > *Is there a relationship between Carol and the narrator?*
   >
   > *What events led to the situation? OR*
   >
   > *What events resulted from the situation?*

2. Verna stood and watched the huge red ball

   slip into the sea. It was a sign of hope. Tomorrow would be a new and brighter day.

Short Story | 59

3. "Can it run?" whispered Jake,

   "We won't know till we try it," answered Troy.

4. After ninety years the Green Orchid was finally home.

   > TRY THREE DIFFERENT PLOTS FOR THE STORY.
   >
   > THE GREEN ORCHID CAN BE
   > 1. A PAINTING
   > 2. A BOAT
   > 3. A PIECE OF JEWELLERY

5. The Tattoo

6. Bailey could not contain his excitement at what he saw under the microscope.

7. The Veil

8. The cat rubbed against his ankles. "Shoo! Mr Tims. It's not supper time."

   Craig bent down to scoop up the cat. He leant closer. There was something in the cat's fur.

9. Write a story based on the picture above.

Generate a variety of ideas. The chart below will help you get started.

Do not settle for the obvious.

Aim for originality.

Short Story

What is that building?
- Think of the past
- old school, former hospital, clinic
- orphanage, ruins of childhood home
- newspaper printery

More about the building!
- Think of the present. What is it now?
- scene of a crime, goal of historical conservation
- smugglers hideout, inheritance, building competition challenge

Who is that man?
- deportee, teacher
- returning emigrant, detective
- GO AHEAD! TRY OTHER IDEAS!

Fig 2.7 Generating ideas from a picture.

 Resources

Search the web for examples of short stories by famous authors.

Try www.online-literature.com for stories by Guy de Maupassant and O. Henry.

3

Descriptive Writing

Descriptive writing helps a reader to imagine a place, a person, a scene an event or an object. It is an attempt to create a picture in words. Descriptive writing appeals to the senses. It aims to create or recreate sights, sounds, smells and textures or touch as well as movement and action.

A strong vocabulary is helpful in giving a good description. You may think that a description will rely only on adjectives. Adjectives are very important in creating a description however other words can aid your description. Adverbs and verbs can be very descriptive as well. A fire can burn **fiercely**. A fire can **rage**. In these examples both the adverb and the verb describe the fire effectively.

Your aim is to make your description vivid. You can use figurative language to make your description strong and vivid. Look at this example. **The road snaked down the hillside.** The metaphor evokes the picture of a dangerously winding road. **He had a snow white halo of hair.** In this case the person's hair encircles his head like a halo. Metaphors, similes, onomatopoeia and personification all can help to give life to a description. You can include colours to aid a visual description. Look at the sentence above again. **He had a snow white halo of hair.** Identify the colour which helps us to see the person's hair.

Where appropriate you may include sounds as well. Get the right words to describe the sounds. **The boom of the ship's horn signalled its departure.** This evokes a loud, deep sound. Here are other examples. **I could hear the click of her heels as she hurried past.**

The water gurgled over the stones.

You will determine the senses to which you will appeal. This will depend on the purpose of the description. A description of a person or a landscape would be mainly visual. Description of a market scene will include sight, sounds and smells. A description of a sporting event will include sight, sounds, action and movement.

As you read books for enjoyment or listen to documentaries pay attention to words and phrases used in descriptions. Jot down those words and expressions which you find interesting and new and vivid.

You will also use descriptive language in your short stories. You will describe the setting of the story and you will use description to create atmosphere. There will be some description of your characters. Sometimes the physical description of a character can be used to suggest the personality of the character.

Here are samples of descriptive writing.

> a) Huge colourful signs - red, green or yellow shouted the names of the shops overhead or at the sides. The shops looked like shoeboxes standing on end. Out of the open ends boxes of goods spilled out onto the sidewalk. A mass of grey-green crabs heaved in a galvanized tub of water. Fish swished lazily in other tubs. Housewives pointed and the shopkeeper netted their choices and imprisoned the fish in plastic bags of water and swung them onto the scales. Deep brown, roasted, chickens hung upside down, dangling from their legs. The lilt and chorus of the strange language swirled all around me.

In sample (a) most of the description is visual.

The writer uses

- colour in the description of the signs, the crabs and the chickens.
- figures of speech. A metaphor is used to show the size and vibrancy of the signs. A simile brings the size and shape of the shops to life.
- sounds in the conversations of the crowd and the tones of the language.

Examine the other samples of descriptive writing below. Identify the methods used to create the description.

b) I looked up at her. Her face was a triangle; the wide brow tapered to a pointed chin. Her nose was small but flat and broad. Her large brown eyes were placed far apart at the outer edges of her face. Their hooded lids made her look like a lizard. I expected her tongue to dart out at me at any moment.

c) The lush green grass grew right down towards the water's edge. The river flowed lazily along as if going for a stroll. The water was as green as the hills and valley above it. On the far side, rounded stones formed a pebbled beach. Between the stones the water gathered in shallow pools. The sun glinted off the still, clear water in the pools. A few long, skinny, wooden canoes glided down the river. A wiry sun browned man sat far back to the stern of one boat. His eyes slanted and squinted against the sun.

d) It has been raining this week like good old fashioned wet season times. The grass on the pastures was lying flat and soggy, beaten down by relentless torrents and swept over by running water making its way somewhere usually towards the roadsides. It was rain that made shouting, splashing boys race coconut shell boats or boats fashioned from a long green blade of grass down the streaming sides of the road. Rain that soaked the outdoor cooking fireplace and made your food cook slowly over a smoky fire as the firewood was wet and water was trying to run through the fireplace. It was the type of rain that meant broken clothes lines under the weight of soggy clothes- clothes that had tried to get dry for three days, beaten by the wind and rendered mute by the rain and finally lying defeated in the mud.

e) The road to the plantation goes decidedly uphill all the way. If you stop to look downhill your eye is caught by the wide sweep of uninterrupted Atlantic Ocean, blue, beautiful and awesome all the way to the horizon. The vegetation is mainly acacia trees, and here and there are tall dark green cactus and lots of thick clumps of long grass. Below and to the right an elongated stretch of pond reflects the sky and the trees at its edge. Suddenly two buildings appear looming out of the vegetation. They stand there - the chimney tall and slender reaching to the sky and the windmill shorter and squat, like husband and wife both strong and silent.

In example (c) the writer uses adjectives and adverbs to create his picture.

In example (d) there is appeal to sight, sound and movement. There is also figurative language.

Passage (e) has a very vivid figurative expression. Identify it.

In addition to the physical description of scenes and people, you will need to describe feelings and emotions. In a short story you will have to describe the emotions of a character. You may have to describe panic, love, fear, anger or reluctance.

Words to describe emotions

Look at the list of emotions in Fig 3.1 and the suggested words and phrases that can be used to describe each emotion.

Fig 3.1 Describing emotions.

anger
- icy stare
- trembling with rage
- voice snapped
- blazing

fear
- quivering, quaking
- numb, petrified, frozen

joy
- heart sang, spirits soared, face beaming
- heart leapt,

Describing physical characteristics

Aim for precise writing in your physical descriptions in order to give your reader a vivid description of the person you are describing. Avoid weak vague words.

Table 3.1 provides examples of words that can be used to describe physical characteristics of persons.

eyes	piercing, sad, darting, slanted, glaring, shifty
smile	engaging, warm, lopsided, mischievous, sly, forced, cold
chin	jutting, blunt, dimpled, pointed, soft, square, strong
beard	straggly, bushy, neat, grizzled,, unkempt, stubble, thick
nose	hooked, flared, thin, long, broad, flat
gait	loping strides, stiff, easy, halting
hair	dreadlocked, wild, tangled, intricately plaited

Table 3.1 Words to describe physical characteristics.

Using figurative language in descriptive writing

You can use a variety of figurative devices to enhance your descriptions. You can begin by using similes.

The children looked neat and tidy. The tidiness could be emphasized with a simile as shown in these two sentences following.

**The boys and girls were clean as freshly scrubbed laundry.
The children looked as crisp as newly harvested lettuce.**

In describing the sound of distant thunder, you can say **I heard the sound of thunder in the distance.** But it can be more vivid to say,

The thunder rumbled in the distance like a giant dog snoring.

Below are samples of descriptive writing in which figurative language is used.

a) The sunlight danced on the bobbing waves. The ferry tucked itself under the overhanging cliffs and rocks and sailed an outstretched hand away from the shore. We passed little pocket handkerchief beaches hemmed in by huge black rocks. Round green hills stood solidly in the background. Passengers awed by the proximity of the vessel to the shore, pointed and gasped at the scenery. The flashing eyes of cell phones winked. Other cameras flashed and whirred but secretly everyone hoped that the captain's sailing skill was infallible.

b) Thunder stuttered nearby while the rain shush-shushed down in soft showers. The gutters swelled into little brown streams rushing empty plastic bottles towards some urgent destination.

Organising the description

You can organise your description spatially to give it order. If you are describing a room you can begin describing the front of the room and then move towards the back as you continue. You can start with the right side of the room moving gradually to the left or vice versa. You can also describe from the floor to the ceiling.

If you are describing a landscape you can start with objects in the foreground and move towards objects in the background or move from the background to the foreground.

If you are describing a person you may start with describing features of his head or face then move to his body then down to his shoes.

You can also choose to begin by describing a particular feature of the face which is special or remarkable or unusual, then moving on to other features.

WRITING WORKSHOP

Activity 3.1

1. Imagine that you have entered a science fair competition and your entry is judged the winner. The prize is a cruise trip to Mexico. Compile a list of words and phrases that you can include in a description of your reaction and feelings upon learning the good news.

   Below are some words to get you started. Continue the list.

   - elated
   - triumph
   - relief
   - rewarding
   - screamed with exhilaration
   - hero
   - confident
   - excitement
   - sleepless with anticipation
   - disbelief
   - pride
   - justified
   - my heart drummed like the beat of the Christmas folk band

2. Make a list of words and phrases that you would use to describe a cane fire or a house fire. Think of all the senses to which you can appeal. Remember to include colour. What do you see? What do you hear? What do you smell? Can you feel anything?

   Look at the sample list below.

hearing & sight
- roar
- crackle
- hiss
- crash of collapsing timbers
- arcing jet of water

smell & sight
- orange flames
- dense black smoke
- acrid
- devouring
- licking at

sight & feel
- lurid glow
- leaping
- dancing
- intense heat
- scorching
- columns of smoke

Descriptive Writing | 71

After you have compiled your list write the description. In your description you can use figurative language. Here are some examples: **"The flames licked at the curtains." "Columns of smoke writhed and twisted towards the sky." "The old warehouse sagged in defeat."**

3. Make a list of similes and metaphors that you would use to describe a stormy, rainy day.

4. Use this list of words to create a descriptive paragraph of 40 words.

- ribbon
- horizon
- glaze
- moonlight
- waves
- molten
- curve
- billow
- sails
- unknown
- captured
- headland
- twinkling lights
- silhouette

5. Match each word or expression in column A with a word or expression from column B to create a vivid description. Some combinations may seem unusual at first. The words can be combined in any order.

Column A	Column B
rain	glared
darkness	sighed
grass	pressed
wind chimes	beaded
heat	silver
door	folds
floorboards	puffed

red bow	chatter
lottery tickets	cooked
breeze	clamoured
pancakes	winked
rumour	tinkled
beach	wandered
phone	shivered
laughter	salty

Be specific

Be specific in your description. Avoid lazy, overused words and expressions. Choose vibrant words which will convey exactly what you want the reader to visualise. Good description depends primarily on your choice of words.

You can vastly improve a sentence such as: **We passed a demonstration on Robert Street.**

Ask yourself a few questions. This will help you to be more specific.

- How did you pass? Did you hurry? Did you have to edge by the demonstration? Or did you push your way through? Could you have threaded your way through the crowd? Squeezed past perhaps? Walked by warily?

Now let us get specific about the demonstration.

- Was it large or small? Can you give an estimate of the size? Was it noisy, rowdy, or violent? Or was it peaceful? Were they waving placards and chanting? Were all the demonstrators female or were they all male?

A more specific sentence could read:

Diane, Paul and I warily hurried past an angry, screaming, mob of hundreds of demonstrators filling the lower end of Robert Street.

The description becomes more vivid with better choice of words.

1. Improve the following sentences to create more vivid descriptions. There are suggestions below some sentences.

    a) A dinosaur was painted on the wall above his bed.
    Think of:
    - the size of the dinosaur
    - colour
    - type of dinosaur
    - posture
    - impression the picture gives.

    b) A very old car drove down the street.

    Appeal to senses. Think of colour, sound, scents.

    Use strong verbs and adverbs and adjectives. Is the car going fast or slowly? Is it progressing steadily or erratically? What is the street like? Is it narrow, bumpy or deserted?

    Try a figure of speech. It could be onomatopoeia, personification, metaphor or simile.

WRITING WORKSHOP

SEE HOW I RAN!

Words to describe RAN:

- Galloped
- Raced
- Flew
- Pitched
- Darted
- Scrambled
- Scampered
- Pounded
- Rushed
- Sped
- Bolted
- Fled
- Sprinted
- Shot
- Jogged
- Scurried
- Dashed
- Hurried
- Darted

c) A fan kept the room cool.
  - Include a sound.
  - Modify the verb
  - Use an adjective to describe the room.

d) I woke to a beautiful day.

e) The boat was on a calm sea.

f) A cat was sleeping on the mat.

g) I knew that the kettle was boiling.

h) The man had a narrow face.

i) I was scared when the lights went out.

j) My house is very unattractive.

k) It rained all day.

l) The teacher wore glasses.

m) I heard the music in the distance.

n) The tour guide climbed up the hill.

Descriptive Writing | 75

2. Describe what you saw on your first visit to a fictional planet.

   Pay attention to the landscape, the light or lack of light, the temperature, the inhabitants or lack of inhabitants. Perhaps there are robots.

3. Describe the scene in the picture below.

4

Summary

A summary gives the main points or the important information derived from a larger body of information. An example would be the information found on the cover of a book which gives a brief idea of the contents of the book.

Another example would be the notes you would take when you are listening to a lecture. It is also the account you give to a friend when he asks about a movie you saw or a class she missed.

You also use the skill when you review a book or article. You would not recount the entire contents of the book. If you represent your club at a conference or meeting, the report you give when you return is an example of a summary. You will not give all the minor details of the meeting. Instead you will give your club members the information that is important and relevant.

Try treating a summary in this way. Imagine that there is someone waiting for a report. Gather and provide the information in which he would be interested.

A summary is an indication that you understand what you read, heard or saw and that you can communicate that understanding. When given written material from which to create a summary read through the material once to understand it. Then read it through again to identify the important points. Collect these points and present them in a coherent or smoothly flowing paragraph. Avoid writing as if you were making a list. Use linking words or transition words to make the writing smooth and connected.

In order to get the main points from written material look at each paragraph. Find the topic sentence. Now you know that you have the main point. Try to identify the type of structure that the writer is using. Is the writer giving advantages or disadvantages? He could also be giving the main causes of an outcome, or the main ways in which a goal is accomplished. He or she could be outlining a process by giving the main steps to be taken in a particular process.

Make notes or underline the areas in the passage that you have identified as important. A writer often gives some information to explain or illustrate the point he is making. Distinguish between the point and the illustration.

In giving a summary

1. Concentrate on repeating the writer's essential point.

2. Generalise the illustrations and examples. Look for similarities and classify.

3. Do not include any new information. Above all do not include your opinion.

4. Do not create an introduction and a conclusion.

5. Be accurate. Do not misrepresent the intention of the author.

6. Keep the same tone as the original passage. Do not change formal writing to an informal tone.

The following are examples of an original paragraph and a sample summary of the paragraph.

a) The forest has traditionally been a source of fuel. Depending on the current level of development of the country, the forest can provide fuel either in the form of charcoal or wood. As long as there is demand for such fuel, providing wood and charcoal can earn money for individuals and families. For many developing countries, wood is still a primary source of fuel. Certainly in the Caribbean, the popularity of barbecues still provides a good market for anyone who can produce the desired charcoal. The price of charcoal has climbed considerably in recent times.

The forest is a source of wood and charcoal for fuel. Persons can earn an income by providing these fuels where there is a strong demand and good prices for them.

b) Aid itself is a complex concept. It can come in so many various forms and they are by no means equal or always effective. Aid can even be destructive despite its well-meaning intent. This is a reference to aid in a more general sense, not the humanitarian assistance given in response to a natural disaster. For international aid to any country to be effective and produce sustainable improvement in the life of people it must be directed at the causes of hardship and poverty and not at the symptoms. Otherwise it will provide a temporary patch at best. Donors in that case will keep wondering why there is no visible progress in relation to the resources provided.

If aid is not directed at the causes of hardship and poverty it will be ineffective in providing a lasting solution.

Generalising examples

If the passage from which you are writing the summary contains many examples make a general statement from the list of details and examples. Find a word or phrase that would categorise or classify the examples.

Here are some sample passages to illustrate how to identify and generalise or categorise the examples used by the writer.

Read passage (a) below.

a) Some persons do not believe that there is such a thing as global warming but there are several signs of unusual natural occurrences. In the Pacific the rising sea level is threatening one island. Glaciers in the Antarctic are melting. The sea temperature is getting hotter and hurricanes are becoming more powerful.

Sentence one is the topic sentence. All the other sentences are examples.

The table below identifies the main idea in the first column and the examples in the second column.

The examples can be classified as signs of global warming. The passage is really saying what is expressed in the topic sentence.

Table 4.1 Identifying examples

Main idea	Example
Some people do not believe in global warming in spite of the signs	In the Pacific rising sea level threatens an island
	Glaciers in the Antarctic are melting
	The sea temperature is getting hotter
	Hurricanes are becoming more powerful

Summary

> **Summary**
>
> Signs of global warming exist though some persons remain sceptical.

Read passage b) below

b) Agricultural production in the Caribbean does not meet the consumers' demand for food. **Droughts, hurricanes, floods and mudslides** often destroy crops and livestock. In addition **tourist resorts, housing estates and new roads and highways** compete with agriculture for the limited available land. Other constraints to increased agricultural production are the periodic outbreaks of pests and diseases such as **the tropical bont tick which infects cattle, the pink mealy bug and the sweet potato weevil.**

You can categorise droughts, hurricanes, floods and mudslides as **natural disasters**.

The tourist resorts, housing estates, new roads and highways can be categorised as **development projects**.

You will see that the writer has categorised the tropical bont tick, the pink mealy bug and sweet potato weevil as **pests and diseases**.

Activity 4.1

1. Read the following short passages and identify the main idea and the examples. Determine what idea the details or examples in a passage are being used to convey.

WRITING WORKSHOP

Then write a summary of each passage using 12 words.

a) West Indian cooks like to add pepper to their dishes. They also rub meats with dry or minced seasonings. The seasoned meats are allowed to rest before cooking for the flavours to penetrate. This makes West Indian food very flavourful and spicy. This food is never bland. Some of the spices are East Indian in origin.

b) Many rural communities live on forest resources. They hunt animals and gather food. Their houses are made from forest materials. Trees give material for shelter. Some of their household articles and implements are made from forest material.

c) The baby will cry. Friends telephone and want to chat. Your brother comes to visit as soon as you are about to get started. Working from home is not easy. Even the neighbour mowing his lawn can be another distraction.

2. At the end of each passage below, four statements are given. Read each passage and select the option that provides the best summary of the passage.

Passage 1

The wetlands are falling victim to the increasing development of previously untouched areas. Marshes are being drained to accommodate business development. Tourism infrastructure such as hotels and marinas are replacing the mangroves. It is generally known that wetlands are invaluable environmental treasures. They are the habitat for a wide variety of animals, insects and birds. Activist groups and individuals work assiduously to sensitise the public on the importance of these natural areas but other concerns about unemployment and poverty often take priority for policy makers.

a) Saving the habitat of birds and insects is of little concern to government officials.

b) Concerns about poverty and unemployment cause policymakers to allow the destruction of wetlands.

c) Environmental activists are unsuccessful in sensitising the public about the importance of wetlands because wildlife habitats are still being destroyed.

d) Unchecked development of the tourism industry is causing environmental degradation.

Passage 2

Migration is one of the most studied aspects of animal behaviour. Birds are most often associated with this type of behaviour. It is less well known that smaller creatures also migrate. Monarch butterflies fly hundreds of miles from Canada to Mexico. Some species of crabs travel overland to the sea at certain times of the year. Even millipedes migrate. The upriver journey of salmon can also be considered an annual migration. Some creatures migrate to find warmer weather while for others it is a part of their mating and reproductive patterns.

a) Scientists concentrated on studying bird migration and have only recently discovered that butterflies and millipedes also migrate.

b) Various species of animals, including birds, migrate either in response to weather patterns or to facilitate their reproduction.

c) Although salmon travel upstream to spawn, their annual journey is not recognised as a form of migration.

d) The study of bird migration far outweighs the study of other types of animal behaviour.

Passage 3

In rural Caribbean villages animals have their roles in the life of the community. A dog is always at the heels of young boys. Cats lie about on shed roofs or on verandas. The animals are often a mixture of both pets and workmates. While they are loved and cared for, animals are expected to contribute to the household. Even the cats, seemingly carefree, are expected to keep the yard and house free of rodents. Dogs provide security services and chase away monkeys from crops and fruit trees. Larger animals such as donkeys and oxen carry loads, pull ploughs and carts and double as a means of transport as well.

a) Villagers in the Caribbean regard some animals as pets while others are used for work.

b) The most useful animals in rural communities are dogs, donkeys and oxen.

c) Animals in rural communities are not kept merely for the pleasure of the owners but serve a useful role in the community.

d) Rural agricultural practices determine the role of animals in the community.

Passage 4

Sibling rivalry can have powerful effects. Younger siblings often compete for the best chair in the room or fight over which television show to watch. Some adults can still remember incidents from their childhood when a sibling manipulated a parent and caused them punishment. Relatives, aware of the jealousy of siblings, are extremely careful when choosing gifts for young nieces and nephews. Some reveal that their strategy is to buy one gift that both children can share, such as a board game. Others buy identical presents for both children even ensuring that the colour is the same. Otherwise, one sibling will try to measure in some way the value of his or her gift against the perceived value of the gift given to his sister or brother.

- a) Adults, aware of the power of sibling rivalry through their own painful memories, go to great lengths to avoid jealousy among their young relatives.

- b) Sibling rivalry affects the young as well as adults, who can retain painful memories of unjust punishment caused by a sibling.

- c) Brothers and sisters always fight when making decisions rather than share possessions.

- d) Sibling rivalry is more powerful than it appears when observed in young children.

Passage 5

For many persons, starting their own business is a dream they hope to achieve. For those who reach their goal, more than fifty percent will fail within five years. Yet small businesses continue to be robust contributors to any economy. In spite of the difficulties, many small business owners prefer the independence of working for themselves. They have to work hard and many spend long hours trying to make their business successful. These entrepreneurs reason that if they could work long hours for an employer then they are more than willing to do so for themselves.

- a) The high failure rate and the hard work associated with small businesses do not deter owners because they value their independence.

- b) It is just as hard to work for an employer as it is to start a business.

c) The dream of owning a small business compensates for the high failure rate.

d) Small businesses are major contributors to any economy despite their high failure rate.

3. Read the following passage in which the writer uses several examples to illustrate the main points of the paragraphs.

a) Complete the table which follows the passage by analysing and summarising the examples used in paragraphs three, four and five.

b) Write a summary of the passage in not more than 120 words.

The green vervet monkey was brought to the West Indies from Africa by French sailors who kept them as pets. This monkey is found on the islands of Barbados and St. Kitts and Nevis. Although cute, the green vervet is in fact an invasive species.

Having no natural enemies on the islands, the monkeys have multiplied to form a large vibrant population. However they have also become a threat to agricultural production and farmers regard them as pests. Fruit crops, vegetables and root crops are all raided by the vervet monkeys as they search for food. Whether the edible parts of the crops are visible or grow underground, the monkeys have the uncanny instinct to discover them. Young, immature crops are often destroyed as well as mature crops ready for harvest. Farmers lose thousands of dollars each year as a result of crop damage by monkeys.

Householders too are now at the mercy of the monkeys which have become bolder and have moved into urban areas. Here they invade backyard gardens eating the fruits and uprooting plants. The monkeys also eat the blossoms of some ornamental plants especially those of the hibiscus and uproot other ornamentals probably out of curiosity. Householders also find it annoying to hear the stomping of the animals on the rooftops and to see them loitering about in the yards and on fences.

Although farmers, especially those with plots on the slopes of foothills in St Kitts and Nevis, have long experienced the incursions of monkeys on their lands, the migration of the animals into suburban areas is more recent. As villas and other housing development expand into previously uninhabited areas, the monkeys are forced to move to new areas to find food. In addition, repeated hurricane damage to the forests has reduced the number of wild fruit sources usually available to the animals. In times of drought too, the vervet monkeys are more frequently seen in the lowlands near human habitation.

There are no easy methods of reducing the green vervet monkey population. Traps can be used but with a large monkey population it would require extensive investment in equipment. Other suggestions are periodic hunting seasons to allow culling of the population. Some persons have even considered contraceptive use to control the rate of increase, though this solution may not be feasible. Planting fruit trees for the monkeys in gullies and marginal lands would provide food for the animals and make them less likely to damage the crops of farmers. Meanwhile the damage to agriculture wrought by monkeys is very costly and their threat to adequate food sources for humans is real.

The examples in paragraph two of the passage above are analysed and summarised in the table below. Complete the table to show analysis and summary of the examples in paragraphs three, four and five.

Table 4.2 Analysing and summarising examples of previous passage.

Paragraph	Analysis of examples	Summary of examples
Two	fruits, vegetables, root crops food above ground or below ready or not for harvesting.	All food crops irrespective of visibility of edible parts and stage of maturity.
Three		
Four		
Five		list methods. impractical or expensive

Taking notes and underlining

You can underline the important points in a passage that you have to summarise. Underlining will help you to focus on what will become the major content of your summary.

You can also choose to take notes of the main points. Read the entire passage first, then read each paragraph and make a note of the main point. If there are examples, make a note of how you will categorise or generalise them.

The use of underlining is illustrated in the example below. The main points are underlined as well as the examples that have to be categorised.

When is a phone smart?

A smartphone is a mobile phone that can do far more than make and receive calls. It is smart because it is more than just another mobile phone. A smartphone wants to be a bit like a computer. *It combines the features of a telephone with some features of a personal computer.* Smartphone users *can access the internet* to send and receive *email messages* on their phones as well as to search for information. Because it can send data and usually has a good quality camera, a smartphone can take and send graduation or wedding *pictures* to distant relatives even *before the ceremony ends.* That is quite smart for just a phone.

The applications or apps are what help to make the phones multi-functional. They are *little computer programs* designed for a single purpose. Apps let you use your smartphone for many additional *purposes not previously associated with a telephone. Because of apps you can do banking on your phone, check the weather, book a hotel room and check your flight status.* Your smartphone makes it possible for you to do all those little but essential tasks while you are away from your home computer. This makes a smart phone convenient - small and convenient.

WRITING WORKSHOP

4. Read the short passage which follows and practise underlining the main points. Then write a summary of the passage in 120 words.

Photographs are treasures for many people. To capture these treasures one can choose either a camera that uses film or a digital camera. Digital cameras have transformed photography. Digital cameras make everybody a photographer, keep friends and families connected and create a large store of memories.

Digital cameras are so easy to use that they can make anyone seem like a competent photographer. Some digital cameras are described as point and shoot. The user just locates the subject and clicks a button. The camera will automatically adjust the focus for the user. The screen which is a feature on many digital cameras lets the user see the picture he is about to take. This would help him to make adjustments to get the picture he wants. Even after he takes the picture he can use the same screen to review the picture. If the person taking the picture is not satisfied he can delete the image and try again. Digital pictures can be viewed on a computer and then can be cropped or even have the colours enhanced. With all that assistance for the user, a digital camera can make a novice seem like an expert photographer.

Another characteristic of digital cameras is the way they help to keep families and friends connected. Pictures taken with a digital camera can be sent almost instantly by email. As a result, pictures of celebrations and special occasions such as graduations, weddings and the birth of a new baby are easily shared with friends and relatives. These pictures make friends and relatives feel closer to one another and more appreciated. Nowadays many people post pictures on social media sites so that those who are close to them can follow or learn of their activities and achievements. Digital cameras make this possible.

Because film is available usually in rolls of 24 or 36, a film camera can only provide just that number of pictures at a time. In contrast a digital camera has enough storage to capture over 100 pictures at a time. The average user would have the ability to create and keep far more memories through photographs than film allowed. In an instant, photographers, whether amateur or professional can produce a large number of pictures to memorialise any occasion, person or even pet.

Activity 4.2

1. **Read the following passage.**

   The populace of the Caribbean has in recent times demanded good governance of their elected officials. They have demanded transparency, accountability and integrity from the politicians. This call has often come from the private sector too. The events in world and regional economies, call for a look at another type of governance – corporate governance. Business leaders are now under the microscope and the same requirements for good governance demanded from governments clearly should be demanded of corporate leaders.

   Corporate governance should also mean integrity, accountability and transparency. Accountability to their shareholders and an interest in the welfare of their customers and other stakeholders are requisites of good corporate governance. Thousands of depositors, investors and other customers of CL Financial, Colonial Life Insurance Company (CLICO) and British American Insurance are in danger of losing their investments and frankly their money. How is it that no one was aware of companies on a wrong path? It is difficult to believe that shareholders would contentedly agree to endanger their own investment. They were clearly ignorant of matters that affected their interest. In the case of the regional companies representatives were giving assurances that CLICO was fine, even while the Trinidad and Tobago government was making efforts to rescue the parent CL Financial.

Businesses should be accountable to the government as well. Indeed, part of corporate governance should be submission to regulation. In the OECS, the banks in the currency union are regulated by the central bank. Insurance companies collect money like banks, but apparently, regulation of these financial institutions was either absent or less stringent. Regulation is only as strong as its enforcement, however. In the Madoff case, the Securities and Exchange Commission of the United States was initially not as vigilant in pursuing suspicious activity noticed by its staff. As a result of the CL Financial troubles, Trinidad and Tobago was urgently making amendments to its 1980 Insurance Act. Things will have to be different in the future as regards regulation.

They have to be. Business leaders were clearly found to be unsatisfactory, to use a very mild term. Deborah Merrill Sands, Dean of the School of Management of Simmons College, Boston says, "These times call for stronger leadership accountability not simply stronger leadership." The Dean calls for "principled leadership" which can be held accountable not only for the short term success of their organizations but also leadership which would measure decisions against a "code of ethics and guiding values and where integrity in decision making is an explicit measure of success." Integrity is as important in business as in public life and a long term view of sustainable success is better than a short term grab for unlikely profits.

A) **Choose from the options below, the statement which best expresses the main point of each paragraph of the passage.**

Paragraph 1

    a) Only governments need to practise good governance

    b) World events are dismal at this time

    c) Public and private sector should exercise good governance

    d. The private sector wants honest governments

Paragraph 2

    a) Customers of CLICO were unaware of the company's failure

    b) Customers and shareholders are stakeholders of a company

    c) Corporations must be accountable to their stakeholders

    d. British American and CLICO are based in Trinidad

Paragraph 3

    a) The Securities and Exchange Commission is inefficient

    b) Trinidad will change its financial regulations

    c) Corporations should face enforced regulations

    d) Madoff was extremely lucky

Paragraph 4

   a) Businesses need stronger leaders
   b) Business leaders should be more ethical
   c) Profits are sometimes uncertain
   d) Short term success is the goal of a business

B) Read the passage above again. Summarise the writer's opinions on corporate governance in not more than 150 words.

Remember to summarise the whole passage. Do not write about the first few paragraphs and then skip over the information given in later paragraphs.

2. Summarising an interview.

Read the entire interview and not just the words spoken by one participant. In this case you are asked to summarise someone's opinions.

Summarise the views of the sports commentator on women's cricket in not more than 60 words.

Interviewer: Mr Brookes, welcome to our programme on Women in Sports. It's good to have a popular sports commentator like you on our show. Let's begin with women's cricket. Many people feel that the women are overshadowed by their male counterparts in this game.

Mr Brookes: Women have been playing cricket for decades now but they just do not seem to be able to attract the same type of attention as the men. Although the women are playing cricket at a very high standard somehow the promoters and organisers of the game give them inadequate attention.

Interviewer: Is this because it is not considered a money-making venture?

Mr Brookes: It can make money if the administrators can sell television rights and attract advertisers.

Interviewer: Are the games appealing enough to draw big crowds

Mr Brookes: The women play very competitively. Their attitude and their skills are at a very high level. Unfortunately many cricket fans have not seen women's cricket at the professional level.

Interviewer: What is the best way to remedy this?

Mr Brookes: A regional competition would help tremendously. Having more competitions similar to those held for the men would attract the attention of the public. If the games are broadcast on radio and television, the public would get the opportunity to judge the quality of the cricket.

Interviewer: What roles should men have in women's cricket?

Mr Brookes: Women can benefit from the long experience of the men in cricket. Men can also help in the areas of coaching, umpiring and administration.

Interviewer: Thank you Mr Brookes and like you I wish women's cricket every success.

3. Summarise the following passage.

   Humming birds are some of the tiniest birds in the world. Most are little more than three inches in length. The smallest known humming bird is the Cuban Bee Hummingbird which is about two inches long and weighs less than an ounce. It is native to Cuba and is not known to exist anywhere else.

The wings of the hummingbirds have unique characteristics. The bird gets its name from the humming sound made by its rapidly beating wings which can beat up to 200 times a second. It is also the only bird which can beat its wings in a circle. This makes it possible for the bird to fly forwards, backwards and sideways. Humming birds can also hover in flight seeming to remain motionless in the air longer than any other bird.

The long tapering beaks of hummingbirds help them to reach inside a flower so that their tongues can extract the nectar. Because these birds feed on nectar from flowers they are important in the process of fertilization of plants. As they feed their beaks transfer pollen from flower to flower. Insects are also part of the diet of hummingbirds.

Hummingbirds are only found in the western hemisphere. They can be found as far north as Alaska and as far south as Chile. They are also found in the West Indian islands. The different locations have different varieties of hummingbirds. In some places, they are called sabrewings or wood nymphs.

Read carefully. Find the important points in each paragraph.

You should have noticed that the writer is concentrating on some characteristics of hummingbirds. These are:

the size of the birds,

the wings and flight,

feeding patterns and

location or habitat.

Read the passage again and make a note of the major facts the writer gives on these characteristics.

Write a paragraph using these major facts to summarise the information given in the article. Make your writing smooth and connected. Use the usual linking words to help you get a flowing paragraph. Use no more than 80 words.

5
Reports

A report is a formal retelling or recounting of an event you witnessed or in which you participated. Reports are commonly used documents in the workplace. A policeman will give a report of a traffic accident, a teacher may be asked to give a report of a field trip organized for her students.

A report is given upon the request of another person. The school's principal can request a report on a playground incident.

A report should state the name and title of the person who will receive the report.

> To: Mrs Hannah Spring
> Principal
> Valley High School
> Montrose

It should have the date when it is prepared.

> To: Mrs Hannah Spring
> Principal
> Valley High School
> Montrose
>
> 25th January 2010

It should have a title which gives a brief indication of the content.

> To: Mrs Hannah Spring
> Principal
> Valley High School
> Montrose
>
> 25th January 2010
>
> Report on Biology field trip for second form, 12th January 2010

Describe the incident you witnessed or the event in which you participated, in chronological order. Ensure that the sequence of events follows logically according to what happened first, then what happened next and so on. Always refer to the date and time of the event. Write the full names of the persons involved. Try to anticipate the questions that the person receiving the report would like to have answered.

As regards the field trip, the principal would like to know the following:

- How many students were taken on the field trip?
- Who accompanied them?
- What was the location of the field trip site or sites?
- What was the purpose of the trip?
- Who received the students at the site?
- What events took place at the site or sites to help the students?

- What were the actions or reactions of the students?
- Did anything unusual occur?
- How did the students conduct themselves?

Here is an example of a report.

To:
Mrs Hannah Spring
Principal
Valley High School
Montrose

25th January 2010

Report on Biology field trip for second form, 12th January 2010

On Wednesday, 12th January 2010 at 2:00 p.m. I took the second form biology class on a field trip to the salt pond at Frigate Bay. The purpose of the trip was to see the variety of life in the pond. There were 20 students in the group and we travelled by bus to the site.

We were received by Mr David Cook, Environment Officer of the Frigate Bay Development Corporation. Mr Cook identified the plant life around the edges of the pond. He also showed the students the examples of birdlife and crustaceans in and around the pond.

The students were very attentive and asked pertinent questions regarding the nesting habits of birds, the size of the pond and the origin of the species of plants and animals seen.

Mr Cook was very knowledgeable and gave valuable information and explanations to the students. We took many photographs of the plant and animal life in and around the pond. Osman Phipps and Samantha Greene were the students designated to take photographs.

The students were allowed to take samples of the pond water for further discovery and investigation in the biology laboratory. These were collected in three small plastic containers.

Karen White thanked Mr Cook and the Frigate Bay Development Corporation for their assistance. We left the site at 3:30 p.m. and returned to the school.

Monica Anchor
Biology Teacher

Note that the report must be signed by the person submitting the report.

Use a formal tone even if the report is based on an informal conversation. Be accurate and give the facts without exaggeration or emphasis.

A report is an important document which is often used by supervisors or other persons in charge to help them make decisions.

Use the full names of persons mentioned in the report. This will help to keep the tone of the report formal and serious.

Format

You can use a format as shown in the sample report.

You can also use a memo format as shown below.

To: Mr Joseph Lucerne, President, Athletic Association, Victoria Road
From: Gillian Masters, President, Speed Queens Athletic Club
Date: 20th February, 2011
Re: Female Athletes Training Camp

A report must show :
- full name and position of recipient
- full name and position of person writing the report
- date when report was written
- subject of the report

A report should not include:
- the opinion of the writer
- recommendations, unless specifically requested

Activity 5.1

1. Read the following conversation. Imagine you are Craig write a report on the talent show for the school's principal.

Beth:	Why are you in such a hurry Craig?
Craig:	I have to get to the library to write a report on the talent show for Principal Fahie.
Beth:	It was a really interesting evening. Thursday 24th June was a night to remember. You should be proud.
Craig	I was the chairperson of the Talent Show Committee. Chad, Gary, Trudie and Chika were the most helpful members.
Beth:	The decorations were gorgeous. They really made the auditorium feel special.
Craig	You have the third formers to thank for that.
Beth:	Why did you choose the Pizza Face band? They seemed as old as my dad but their music was great.
Craig:	After our first choice cancelled their appearance at the last moment, the Pizza Face was willing to help us at such late notice. The Moving Mangoes let us down. They said that they were practising for an album recording. Their schedule had become crowded so they could not play for us.
Beth:	Well we didn't miss them. All the other high schools supported us. The auditorium was packed long before the start time of 8 o'clock. I was surprised to see so many students from other high schools.
Craig:	Well Chika worked hard on the publicity. She handed out flyers outside the schools. Morris High and Star Academy let us put posters on their notice boards.
Beth:	I think the acts were great. I enjoyed the comedians the best, but the dancing and singing were a close second. I had no idea we had such talent at Croton High.
Craig:	Yes and it was all worth the effort. We collected $5000. It is more than enough to buy the projector for the Learning Centre. Principal Fahie will be pleased.
Beth:	Well get that report to him on time.

2. You are the leader of a debating team which travelled to Holland to participate in a debating competition. The team reached the finals in its category but lost to its opponents. Below are the notes you made about the competition. Using the notes write a report you would submit to the principal of your high school.

Tuesday 20th September: Arrived airport safely. Team tired after long flight. No bags lost.
Hotel comfortable but we waited hours to get rooms. Rooms not ready.
Wednesday 21st September: Our team debating tonight at 8:00 against New Zealand. We got
the proposition. Maxine and Kumar will debate. Will have to be sharp. New Zealand boys
Darren and Colin are tough - handsome too.
Thursday 22nd September: We won. We're through to the next round. Difficult to argue that
cell phones encourage anti-social behaviour in teenagers. We barely managed. 434 points to
430. Kumar's rebuttal solid. Got best speaker for that too. One day only to practise for next
round. Have to use Shauna and Marcel - our best. Must beat Ireland for semi-finals.
They just clobbered England. Unexpected but they were very good. Sight-seeing tomorrow.
Morning only. Hope twelve of us fit in tour bus. Have to remember sales tax.
Friday 23rd September: Problems, problems. Shauna getting a cold, throat hurts. Got Frank to
practise just in case. He doesn't like it. Not much time to prepare him. Hours to go. We're
scrambling. Opposing this time.
Saturday 24th September: Frank was very good. Big scores 480 to Ireland's 470. No prizes
though. Best two for finals Kumar and Shauna. Supporting alternative energy as best for

> *environment easier than opposing. No sightseeing, no shopping. Preparation all day.*
>
> *Australia is defending champion - confident team, rebuttals strong. Hard work for us.*
>
> *Sunday 25th . Finals. Disappointing performance . Lost by 12 points 460 to 472. Have*
>
> *runner-up trophy. Still did well considering.*

WRITING TIPS

Organise your writing.

Sort your ideas. Put related ideas together

Decide on the order in which you will present your information.

How will you start?

What will come next?

Decide how you will conclude.

Make this plan before you begin writing.

Organising your writing will help you to communicate clearly and achieve the purpose of your writing.

3. Read the following passage. Imagine you are Marlene and write a report on the situation for the legal department.

Marlene Singh, office manager at Anansi Productions Ltd, bought a laser colour printer for the marketing and promotions department from a company called Office Solutions. The department was very happy with the printer for the first six weeks. It was fast. The promotion materials were crisp and vibrant.

Then Jerry Herbert, marketing assistant, brought some samples of printed materials to Marlene. Jerry showed her the smudged words and graphics. The quality of the marketing materials was poor and could not be distributed to the public. Jerry also explained that the problems with the printer were causing the company to lose money. They were wasting materials trying to get the printer to produce and losing money because of the inability to accomplish marketing goals.

Marlene asks Office Solutions to replace the faulty printer. Office Solutions refuses. The sales clerk claims that the printer's warranty has expired and in any case the fault must have been caused by the users at Anansi Productions. Marlene refers the matter to Carl Letsome the sales supervisor at Office Solutions. She reminds him that her company is a loyal customer of Office Solutions and has conducted valuable business worth tens of thousands of dollars with them over several years.

Mr Letsome, promises to send one of his technicians to Anansi Productions to check the printer. He advises Marlene that his decision on further action will depend on the technician's report. At this point Marlene decides to write a report to the legal department of Anansi Productions.

4. You left a bag containing several important documents on a bus owned by the National Transportation Ministry. Write a letter to the Director of Transportation reporting your loss. Be sure to include all necessary information that would assist in recovery of your property.

5. Your friend Janine has found a job as a high school teacher in your country and has to move there in a few weeks. She has written to you asking you to recommend suitable accommodation. She is twenty years old and single and would like to live close to her place of work or close to public transportation. She is interested in a secure location but wants accommodation that is reasonably priced.

Janine reminds you that she still plays netball and wants to maintain her exercise routine. She values her privacy and is not interested in having a roommate or sharing any facilities with other tenants except perhaps laundry facilities.

Write a letter to Janine in no more than 120 words recommending suitable accommodation that would satisfy her requirements and personality. Give her the relevant information that would help her make a decision.

6. Correct the following report paying attention to format, organisation and relevance of content.

To: Mrs Mabel Crystal, Principal, Shoretown High School

From: Scott Payne, Captain

On Friday 14th our team was playing a match against the Mavericks of Salt Rock High School. We beat them last year in the Championships. Anyway the game started late because of transportation difficulties. The bus that we used was just too old and too slow. It was a green bus. When we arrived at Maynard's Park the officials were almost ready to cancel the game. They threatened to disqualify our team. I did not think that this was fair because we were not responsible for the poor condition of the bus.

After Coach Alexander spoke with them we were allowed to play. Mr James and Mr Questal are very strict officials. But we were there in less than hour after the game should have started so they could not disqualify us. That is why we appealed when they changed their decision after the game. We had just won. The score was three goals for us and one to the Mavericks. I think it was poor sportsmanship to reverse their decision after we had won.

Fortunately for us Mr Rudolf, our team manager, knows all the rules of the game. He registered a protest with the National Football Association. We will have a hearing on the 31st October to appeal against the disqualification. I think we will be successful. I think that the adults should have displayed a better example of sportsmanship in the presence of the students. Many of the boys were angry especially Steve and Rahim. They started shouting but our coach insisted on discipline and respect. There was no fighting. We get to speak at the hearing.

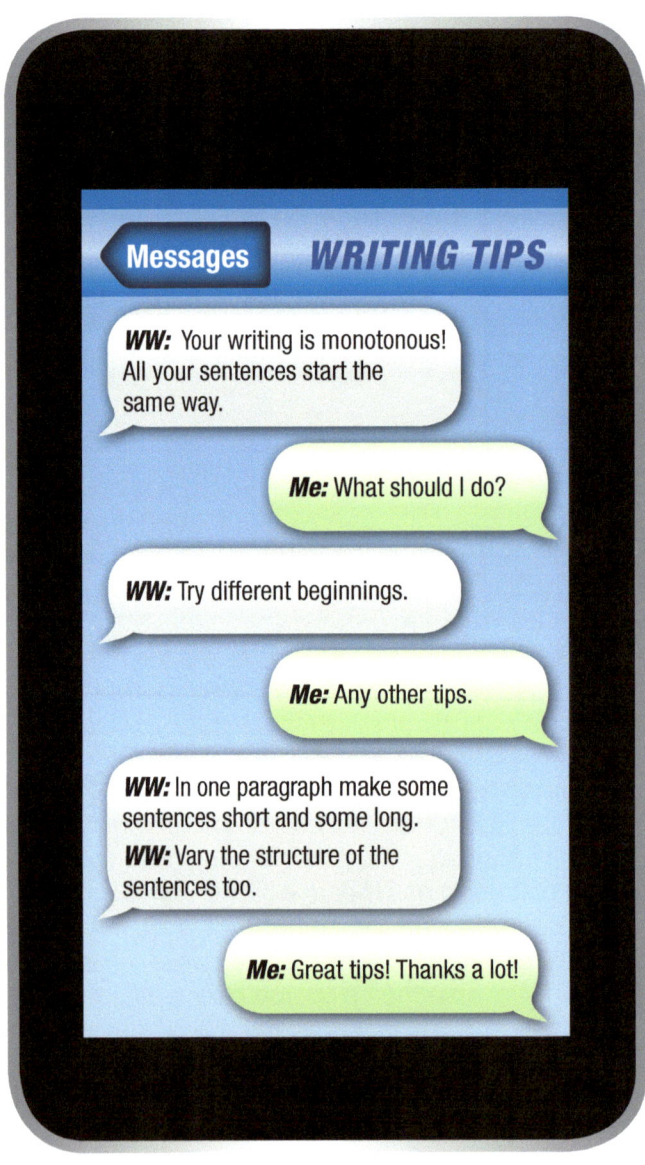

About the Author

Terry Nisbett was first published when Nelson included her story *The Hummingbird and the Hibiscus* in Book 4 of Nelson Caribbean Readers. She has also published articles in *Federations* magazine and in *Americas,* the magazine of the Organisation of American States. Currently she writes regularly for the *Daily Herald* of St Martin. She has been teaching writing for more than 30 years to high school students, undergraduates and adults continuing their education.

Terry Nisbett is a former Head of Division of the Faculty of Arts Science and General Studies of the Clarence Fitzroy Bryant College and former Principal of the Charlestown Secondary School. She has participated as an Assistant Examiner for CXC for English A on numerous occasions. She now combines her tutoring and marketing consultant business with her freelance writing

www.ingramcontent.com/pod-product-compliance
Lightning Source LLC
Chambersburg PA
CBHW040052160426
43192CB00002B/49